CASS SERIES ON THE SOVIET STUDY OF WAR NO. 1

SOVIET DOCUMENTS ON THE USE OF WAR EXPERIENCE

VOLUME I
The Initial Period of War 1941

CASS SERIES ON THE SOVIET STUDY OF WAR
(Selected Translations)

Series Editor – David M. Glantz
Ft. Leavenworth, Kansas

This series examines what Soviet military theorists and commanders have learned from the study of their own military operations. Separate volumes contain annotated translations of Soviet works analyzing their war experiences as well as the works of important Soviet military theorists and collections of Soviet articles concerning specific campaigns, operations, or military techniques.

SOVIET DOCUMENTS ON THE USE OF WAR EXPERIENCE

VOLUME ONE

The Initial Period of War 1941

Translated by
HAROLD S. ORENSTEIN
Soviet Army Studies Office
Combined Arms Center, Fort Leavenworth, KS

With an Introduction by David M. Glantz

Routledge
Taylor & Francis Group

LONDON AND NEW YORK

First published 1991 in Great Britain by
FRANK CASS & CO. LTD

Published 2015 by Routledge
2 Park Square, Milton Park, Abingdon, Oxfordshire OX14 4RN
711 Third Avenue, New York, NY 10017

First issued in paperback 2015

Routledge is an imprint of the Taylor and Francis Group, an informa business

British Library Cataloguing in Publication Data
 Soviet documents on the use of war experience.
 Vol. 1.
 1. World war 2 : Military operations
 940.541247

Library of Congress Cataloging-in-Publication Data

Soviet documents on the use of war experience / translated by Harold
 S. Orenstein ; with an introduction by David M. Glantz.
  2 v. ; c.m. -- (Cass series on the Soviet study of war ; no. 1–2)
  Translated from the Russian.
  Includes bibliographical references.
  Contents: v. 1. The initial period of war, 1941, -- v. 2. The
 Winter Campaign 1941–1942.
  ISBN 0–7146–3392–5 (v. 1). -- ISBN 0–7146–3393–3 (v. 2)
  1. World War, 1939–1945--Campaigns--Soviet Union. I. Orenstein,
 Harold S. (Harold Steven), 1948– . II. Series.
 U740.S68 1991
 940.54′1247--dc20
                  91–11452
                    CIP

ISBN 13: 978-1-138-88191-4 (pbk)
ISBN 13: 978-0-7146-3392-3 (hbk)

Typeset by Selectmove Ltd

CONTENTS

INTRODUCTION

The Soviet Use of War Experience

CONTEXT

On the morning of 22 June 1941 Nazi Germany unleashed a sudden and massive offensive aimed at destroying the Soviet state. The ambitious German undertaking, based on the premise that the bulk of the Red Army could be annihilated in the immediate border regions by use of a large-scale blitzkrieg, caught the Soviets only partially prepared for war. Force reconstruction and re-equipment programs were underway but incomplete, and, although the Soviets had ample warning, for as yet inexplicable reasons Stalin forbade the Soviet military from taking prudent defensive precautions, thus granting the Germans the benefits of strategic, operational and tactical surprise. German hammer blows staggered the Soviet armed forces and almost destroyed them. By Soviet admission:

> our pre-war views on the conduct of armed struggle in the initial period of war did not investigate the possibility of concealed timely deployment and simultaneous enemy armed forces operations on the land, in the air and at sea. Mistakes in theory had a negative effect on resolving the practical questions of covering the state borders and deploying the armed forces, which, along with other reasons, caused serious misfortunes in the war.
>
> There were many problems in working out command and control and organizing communications with operational large units. The assertion that the defense found fullest expression only in the realm of army operations was incorrect, as was the view that the struggle for air superiority must be realized on the scale of *front* and army operations. The complicated views at the beginning of the war concerning the organization of the army and forces' rear did not fully answer the demands of the theory of deep offensive operations and battle. Operational and forces' rear services remained cumbersome and immobile.
>
> There were also serious deficiencies in the theoretical training of commanders and in the combat training of forces. . . .[1]

These Soviet admissions, as frank as they were, understated the scale of the problem. In the initial months of the war, Soviet commanders at higher levels demonstrated an ineptness only partially compensated for by the fervor of junior officers and the stoicism and bravery of the hard-pressed troops. *Front* and army commanders were unable to construct coherent defenses against the German armored thrusts and displayed an alarming propensity for launching costly uncoordinated counter-attacks predestined to failure. Only looming disaster drove the Soviet High Command to action in a war which quickly became one of survival.

Ultimately the Red Army successfully met this great challenge and triumphed, but only after years of attrition, frustration, and an agonizing process of military re-education conducted during wartime. Throughout the war a new generation of commanders emerged, new equipment was developed and fielded, and military theories matured after their late 1930s hiatus. In essence, the concept of deep operations, so dominant in the early 1930s, in fact if not in name, became the focal point of Soviet offensive theory and the means of converting tactical success into operational and, ultimately, strategic success. By late 1943 Soviet military theory and the Soviet force structure were wed into a successful formula for achieving victory. During the ensuing two years of war the Soviets experimented with operational techniques, refined their force structure, and worked to overcome resource and logistical constraints. This second great renaissance in Soviet military thought, which built upon the first renaissance of the 1930s, is ignored in the West today because it was overshadowed by the Soviet disasters of 1941 and 1942, which were thoroughly covered in the post-war works of victorious German generals. Today, however, that renaissance is viewed by the Soviets as the most important period in Soviet military affairs, a vast laboratory for military analysis and a repository of experience that can be and is tapped for inspiration and concrete advice when addressing contemporary and future military problems.

For the sake of analysis the Soviets subdivide their "Great Patriotic War" into three distinct periods, each characterized by broad unifying themes reflecting Soviet fortunes in war and the state of military art.[2] The first period (June 1941–November 1942) found the Soviets on the strategic defense punctuated by Soviet attempts to undertake offensive operations on several important axes. The second period (December 1942–December 1943) was one of transition from defensive operations to a general Soviet offensive designed to wrest the strategic initiative from the Germans. The third period (1944–45) was a period of general Soviet offensives culminating in the achievement of total victory.

The first and most difficult period commenced in June 1941 with the German invasion and the series of border battles during which the Germans swallowed up large segments of deployed Soviet forces amounting to as much as 50 per cent of the Soviet peacetime army. The large-scale encirclements of Soviet forces at Minsk, Smolensk, Kiev, Briansk, and Viaz'ma culminated in the fall of 1941, when German forces tried to cap their victorious advance with the seizure of Moscow by one final envelopment. The German failure to take Moscow prompted the first major Soviet attempt to regain the strategic initiative. A desperate Soviet winter offensive in the Moscow environs broadened into an attempt to expand the offensive across the front from Leningrad to Rostov and the Crimea, but foundered because of insufficient Soviet forces and materiel, and left the Soviets vulnerable to renewed German strategic thrusts in the summer of 1942. The ill-fated and costly Soviet offensive failures at Khar'kov and Kerch in May 1942 were followed by a general German offensive in southern Russia, which, by late fall, had reached the Volga River at Stalingrad and the passes of the Caucasus Mountains. As with the 1941 German offensive effort, by late fall the Germans were overextended, even as the Soviets again husbanded their resources for a major counteroffensive. Unlike 1941, in 1942 the Soviets undertook organizational measures and theoretical studies to better parry the German offensive as it lost momentum on the banks of the Volga. The Soviet November offensive around Stalingrad saw the strategic initiative pass into Soviet hands and marked the end of the first period of war.

SYSTEMATIC USE OF WAR EXPERIENCE

Even before the outbreak of the Second World War, Soviet military theorists and practitioners, working within the General Staff, appreciated and exploited both Soviet and foreign war experiences. In the 1920s a host of military theorists pondered the lessons of the World War, the Russian Civil War, and the Russo-Polish War as they sought to define military doctrine, military science, military art and force structure of the Red Army. While the work of such distinguished theorists as Frunze, Svechin, Triandafillov, and Tukhachevsky dominated military historiography, numerous other writers contributed to what, in essence, was the beginning of a renaissance in Soviet military thought. That renaissance and associated study subsequently gave birth to the Soviet concepts of deep battle and deep operations, which dominated Soviet military thought at the tactical and operational levels in the 1930s.

Further intense study of war experience went hand in hand with field and practical exercises in the early and mid-1930s as the Soviets implemented a motor-mechanization program for their armed forces. The Soviets created a variety of mechanized, armored and air assault units suited to implement their emphasis on tactical and operational maneuver, which so dominated Soviet military science. Study of past wars and contemporary peacetime exercises provided a litmus test for the validity of new tactical and operational concepts and forces created to carry them out.

Soviet analysis of war experience continued unchanged throughout the 1930s, although the quality of that analysis and Soviet willingness to respond imaginatively and effectively to it wilted as a result of the ensuing purges of the Soviet military. Of central concern to Soviet theorists was the validity of concepts enumerated in their Field Service Regulation of 1936, which spelled out how deep battle was to be conducted. That regulation postulated reliance on offensive combat and the early and extensive employment of armored and mechanized forces to both initiate and develop deep maneuver. Hence the military experience of conflicts which broke out in the late 1930s provided a ready forum for testing current advanced Soviet concepts.

Soviet writings in a variety of journals and newspapers accurately reflected the quantity and quality of war experience analysis going on within the General Staff. While continuing their analysis of earlier operations, Soviet theorists now turned their attention to ongoing conflict in the Far East and Spain. The Spanish Civil War had special importance because of the significant role played in it by modern weaponry, in particular tanks and aircraft, which were employed extensively by both sides. A series of articles published in the Red Army newspaper *Krasnaia zvezda* [Red Star] focused on the nature of combat in Spain, and by late 1937 and 1938 evidenced growing Soviet uncertainty over the validity of their 1936 regulations. Admittedly the post-1937 purges also dampened Soviet enthusiasm for new concepts and new ideas.

If the purges had a negative effect in 1938 and 1939, this was not readily apparent in subsequent analysis of combat in the initial phases of the Second World War. Soviet analytical articles published in the General Staff journal *Voennaia mysl'* [Military Thought] and in *Voenno-istoricheskii zhurnal* [Military Historical Journal] during 1940 and 1941 were of the highest quality and clearly demonstrated that the Soviet military understood both the importance of emerging German blitzkrieg concepts and the relevance of these concepts vis-à-vis the Soviet military itself. Although equally candid public analysis of Soviet failures in Finland and Poland was not apparent, the inference is that such studies were being done within the General Staff.

One can debate the merits and impact of Soviet study during the pre-1941 period, for clearly the purges, which ripped the heart, brain, and soul out of the military, had a damaging effect on the analysis itself and, more importantly, on the Soviet ability to react positively on the basis of that analysis. Whatever progress the Soviets had achieved was clearly negated by the devastating German attack of 22 June 1941 and the perilous period which followed immediately thereafter.

A contemporary Soviet military theorist has written:

> As is well known, the Great Patriotic War began in conditions unfavorable for the Soviet Union. A surprise blow of a multi-million-man, fully mobilized, and well-equipped German-Fascist army, which had almost two years of combat experience in military operations, fell upon our nation. To a large degree this anticipated the unfortunate outcome of the initial period of war and several subsequent operations for the Soviet Army. The reason for these misfortunes is a theme of special discussion. Of major importance among them was the absence in our forces of combat practice.[3]

This blunt statement emphasized the dilemmas faced by a nation preparing its army for war, and underscored again the critical role played by combat experience in armed forces preparedness. Soviet inability to deal with the massive German invasion had grave consequences for the Soviet military and state and, in fact, almost led to the destruction of both.

The Soviets, however, responded to the crisis in practical fashion. In mid-July 1941 the *STAVKA* [High Command] and General Staff dispatched to operating forces groups of senior officers to analyze the nature of combat and recommend remedies to apparent problems. Simultaneously the General Staff required the chiefs of staff of strategic directions, *fronts*, and armies to collect and forward to the General Staff

> all materials reflecting the combat experience of our forces and new combat techniques of enemy forces, and conclusions and proposals on the organization, armament and combat use of units and formations, on the preparation and conduct of battles and operations, and on command and control of forces and their all round protection.[4]

A subsequent order of the People's Commissariat of Defense, issued on 25 April 1942, established a system of organs to gather and use war experience from the General Staff through army level. This order, however, was only partially implemented and produced uneven results. Consequently in November 1942 the *STAVKA* issued a new order which addressed the weaknesses in its predecessor and established a firm system for collecting, analyzing, and exploiting war experiences. Immediately thereafter the Soviet military began harnessing that system in the service of the entire armed forces.

THE WARTIME SOVIET WAR EXPERIENCE ANALYSIS SYSTEM

The following document is taken from Volume Two of a classified Soviet publication entitled *Sbornik materialov po izucheniiu opyta voiny* [Collection of Materials on the Study of War Experience] (Moscow: Voenizdat, 1943). It is the order which articulated Red Army problems and mandated the creation of the machinery necessary to solve the problems through implementation of the process for studying and exploiting war experiences.

Subsequent to this order the Soviets fully implemented the system and ultimately produced over 60 volumes of detailed analysis of all aspects of operations. This analysis served as a basis for adjustments in Soviet force structure and for the development of new operational and tactical combat techniques. The volumes also provided materials for use in journal articles, military analyses, and post-war military operational studies.

The system inaugurated by the November 1942 order has endured, and the Soviets presently use it to analyze the experiences of foreign armies in local wars and the Soviet Army in the recent Afghan conflict. Current Soviet analytical writings reflect this system for the analysis of war experiences and are direct products of it.

Directive of the General Staff Concerning the Study and Application of War Experience

Directive No 1005216   9 November 1942

To the Chiefs of Staff of *Fronts* and Armies:

A survey has revealed that in most *front* and army staffs the work of studying the experience of the war is not satisfactorily conducted. The staffs of the Western and Northwestern Fronts, and those of a few armies, are paying more than average attention to the matter, but in general this work is not being properly planned nor carried out on the necessary scale. The main shortcoming is the failure to convey properly and in useful form, and in a timely manner the results of war-experience studies to the troops.

The chiefs of staff of *fronts* and armies and the chiefs of operations sections, as a rule, do not attempt to study and draw general conclusions from the study of war experience. In many cases they appear to consider that this is a job for future historians, and reckon that by keeping combat journals they have done all that is necessary. This incorrect view on their part as to the value of the study of war experience leads to the repetition by commanders and troops of the same mistakes over and over in the organization and conduct of combat, and it slows down the process of communicating to the troops new combat procedures and the use by the troops of these procedures in combat.

Specially designated officers have been assigned to the staffs of *fronts* and armies since last April, when T/O positions for such officers were created in the operations section of those staffs. In this connection, it has been discovered that in many cases the T/O position of assistant to the chief of the operations section for the study of war experience has not yet been filled, and, in a number of cases where the position has been filled, the officer concerned is not being used for the intended purpose. The assistants to the chiefs of operations sections for the study of war experience are being used for all kinds of casual work having no connection with their task as stated in the T/O. Thus, the captain who was assigned to this position in the 64th Army on 5 June had not yet begun his assigned task by 27 September. And the assistant to the chief of the operations section for the application of war experience, a senior lieutenant, was also doing work that had nothing to do with his basic assignment. Similar instances can be cited in the cases of various other armies (29th, 5th, 30th, 1st Air) and *fronts*.

Front and army staffs have no plans for the generalization of war experience; they do not exchange the results of war experience study with neighboring *fronts* and armies. Critiques of operations are conducted in a perfunctory and pro-forma manner so that officers attending the critiques derive little benefit from them. Units subordinate to *fronts* and armies – active units and particularly reserve units – are hardly informed concerning new combat methods and procedures (29th, 5th, 64th, and 30th Armies have a particularly bad record). Often the reports and conclusions concerning war experience prepared by the General Staff are either not disseminated down, or the dissemination involves only excerpts or watered-down résumés. The operational résumés presented at the General Staff in Moscow often contain little useful generalization concerning operational questions, and concrete conclusions and recommendations concerning combined-arms tactics and infantry tactics are made far too rarely.

The staffs of *fronts* and armies are weak in their direction of lower staffs in the study and use of war experience.

It is essential to:

1. By 25 November of this year, choose the most capable officer possible, who will be able competently to study and summarize war experience, and in each *front* and army appoint him to the T/O position of assistant to the chief of the operations section for the study of war experience. The T/O calls for a chief assistant, aided by several assistants. All positions will be filled.

2. Categorically prohibit these officers from undertaking any tasks other than those which their T/O position provides. They must be freed from all other duties, and given full scope to accomplish their basic tasks.

3. Immediately on receipt of this directive, draw up in *front* and army staffs a plan for the study of war experience, indicating specifically, in terms of the particular problems most urgently facing each army and *front*, the priority of operational and tactical questions to be studied. This plan must cover the period up to the end of the year.

4. This plan, with its list of priority matters for study, and with a list of the officers assigned to war experience study, will be submitted by 25 November 1942 to the General Staff in Moscow, through the General Staff Section for the Study of War Experience, by each *front* and army HQ.

5. Chiefs of staff will direct the work of the officers conducting studies of war experiences, and will afford them practical assistance personally and through their chiefs of operational sections. The latter must review daily the work of their assistants for the study of war experience.

6. Information will be systematically published concerning war experience, and this material will be utilized widely through indoctrination of troops and reserve units and second-echelon units, through distribution to officers and staff personnel, through exchange of combat experience information between neighboring armies and *fronts*, and through improvement in the quality of critiques carried out by staffs after the completion of an operation or of a phase of an operation (these critiques will be carried out at all levels).

7. By the 20th of each month a report will be submitted to the Section of the General Staff in Moscow for the Study of War Experience containing a brief summary of the generalizations and conclusions arrived at for the preceding month. The summary and conclusions will be supported by appropriate diagrams, tables, figures, and salient facts concerning operations and combat actions on the basis of which conclusions are drawn. In the summary, in addition to a consideration of the operational employment of troops, there will be clarifications and comments concerning the combat employment of all types of weapons, enemy as well as friendly. In cases of especially noteworthy observations or discoveries concerning combat methods or the combat employment of weapons, a detailed report should be submitted immediately, without waiting for the regular monthly report.

8. *Front* and army staffs must immediately digest and be guided by the attached brief "Instruction Concerning the Study and Application of War Experience." This instruction must be transmitted to subordinate staffs and to all persons engaged in the study of war experience.

9. The Chief of the Section for the Study of War Experience of the General Staff of the Red Army will check the work of *front* and army staffs in his field, and will afford all possible aid and assistance.

Approved:
Deputy Chief of the General Staff of the Red Army
Maj Gen BOKOV   10 Nov. 1942

Inclosure:

Instruction Concerning the Study and Application of War Experience in *Front* and Army Staffs

I. GENERAL PRINCIPLES

1. The timely study, generalization, and application of war experience is an important task of all commanders and staffs.

    The analysis, generalization, and application of war experience enables the troops to:

    - improve the organization and conduct of combat, overcome shortcomings, and avoid errors committed in previous actions and operations;
    - make the best use of the full power of the armament and equipment of the various arms on the basis of tried and tested methods of cooperation and of massed and decentralized employment;
    - by employing new proven methods of combat, achieve surprise, which is one of the most important elements of success in combat;
    - by being warned concerning the enemy way of using new arms and new equipment, avoid being surprised thereby.

2. All work on the study, analysis, generalization, and application of war experience will be centralized and will be conducted by *front* and army staffs. Present T/Os provide the following working apparatus to accomplish this task:

    - in the *Front* Field HQ, one senior assistant and three assistants to the Chief of the Operations Section for the Study of War Experience;
    - in the Army Field HQ, one senior assistant and one assistant.

    The basic task of these working groups is, under the orders of the chief of staff and under the direct supervision of the chief of the operations section, to carry out on a daily basis for the entire command the collection, study, and generalization of war experience, and to make timely distribution to the troops by various media of the generalizations and conclusions.

II. DUTIES OF THE PERSONS RESPONSIBLE ON STAFFS FOR THE STUDY OF WAR EXPERIENCE

(Army and *Front* Staffs)

3. *Chief of Staff* – On the order of the commander, he exercises overall supervision of the study of war experience, and facilitates the dissemination of the results thereof so that it can be used in the training of troops, officers, and staffs.

He indicates to the chief of the operations section the basic operational and tactical matters which should particularly be studied; he reviews and approves the plan for the study of war experience; and he facilitates the flow of information from the chiefs of the arms and services and their chiefs of staff and officers on matters of particular importance for current war experience studies.

4. *Chief of the Operations Section* – He personally supervises the work of the chief (senior) assistant for the study of war experience. He personally, or through his senior duty, must:

- prepare detailed requirements for war experience study based on the experience of each of the arms, and of each of the major formations of the command;
- prescribe the form in which the results of the war experience study will be disseminated, whether by published papers, or critiques, or exercises for staff officers or officer groups, or by brief summary-and-conclusion type reports;
- maintain close liaison with the chief of the combat training section, so that he can quickly inform him of any significant conclusions derived from war experience study that should be incorporated into the training program of troop units and reserve units.

5. *Senior Assistant to the Chief of the Operations Section for the Study of War Experience* – He is responsible for:

- organizing the collection of war experience data from the troops and the staffs that are subordinate to the *front* or army to which he is assigned;
- together with the reconnaissance (intelligence) section, studying and drawing conclusions concerning enemy combat methods, while on the lookout for any new enemy types of materiel or weapons (or ways of employing weapons) that might introduce an element of surprise if they were used without our troops having been warned about them;
- studying war experience and drawing conclusions from his study, the study and conclusions being presented with appropriate text, charts, figures, etc. to the chief of the operations section;
- compiling, on the orders of the chief of the operations section, the working plans for the study of war experience. A quarterly overall plan is prepared, as well as a monthly detailed plan, showing the schedule of work and the particular operations or phases of combat that are to be treated;
- on the orders of the chief of the operations section, drawing up directives, orders, and instructions concerning changes in combat methods which the results of his study show to be desirable;
- assigning to subordinate staffs and to the chiefs of the arms and services specific tasks involving the study of war experience or the checking of facts bearing on such study;
- bringing to the attention of the troops all new information which results from his studies, such information to be disseminated in the particular form ordered by the chief of the operations section; and informing neighboring units as well;
- compiling monthly reports containing the basic data and most significant conclusions derived from his studies;

- guiding the work of his assistants by means of individual conferences with them concerning their assigned projects for the study of operational and tactical matters as they affect the work of the troops and of staffs.

III. PLANNING AND METHODS OF WORK

6. The overall plan of an army or *front* staff for the study of war experience is compiled on a quarterly basis. It includes:

    - questions of an operational and tactical character, involving both our forces and enemy forces, that need to be subjected to detailed and long-term analytical study;
    - study of the characteristics of the actions of the various arms and services in the particular theater in which the command is operating, with special attention to winter conditions and to conditions during the muddy period of the spring thaws and autumn rains;
    - a timetable showing when periodic or special documents such as directives, reviews, collections of generalized studies, etc. must be issued;
    - the actual individuals, by name, such as formation or unit commanders, staffs, staff sections, individual staff officers, etc. who have been assigned tasks relating to the study of war experience, and the deadlines for the completion of each of these tasks.

    This overall quarterly plan is approved by the chief of staff of the *front* or army.

    Note: The overall three-month plan of the army will be based on that of the *front*; appropriate parts relating particularly to the army in each case will be developed in greater detail.

7. The monthly plan is the operations section's working document for the study of war experience. It includes:

    - the deadlines for current work, with indications also of deadlines for the submission of material in written form from other staff elements or lower echelons, and specific indication of who is responsible for the submission of such written materials;
    - a list of the materials that will have to be prepared in order to satisfy the requirements for officers' courses and meetings, CPXs, command and staff field expeditions (generally like tactical walks), critiques, and troop training;
    - the deadline, place, and name of the person responsible for checking various tactical procedures and methods of employment of weapons and materiel on the basis of specific experience in given units and formations.

    The monthly plan of work is approved by the chief of the operations section.

8. The plan of work for the study of combat experience based on a specific operation is drawn up at the time the given study is undertaken. It includes a brief résumé of the matters particularly to be studied, such as, for example, the planning of the operation (or action), the organization of cooperation, the

regrouping and relief of troops, the use of radio in the control and direction of the troops, etc.

This plan also serves as the outline for a brief summary that will later be written up concerning the given operation.

9. The senior assistant to the chief of the operations section for the study of war experience organizes and conducts his work in the following ways:

- on the orders of the chief of the operations section, he prepares requests for information and data addressed to subordinate staffs, chiefs of the arms and services, and chiefs of other staff sections. After these are signed by the chief of staff, he (the senior assistant) delivers them to the persons who will be responsible for answering them;
- on the eve of an operation to be carried out by formations and units of his *front* or army, he or his assistants personally visit the sector where the operation is to take place, so as to observe the specific parts of the operation which he will have to study as part of his planned work;
- when necessary, and with the approval of the chief of staff, he appoints, instructs, and sends to the front teams of officers to study enemy defense systems, enemy defense works which have been overrun, and captured enemy materiel. He organizes the work of such special teams so that they will submit not only a written report, but also sketches, drawings, diagrams, photos, etc., that will support their report and their conclusions;
- on a daily basis he keeps up with the combat situation by following combat reports, reading combat documents, including operational summaries, the combat journals of his staff and of lower staffs, summaries, résumés, etc. From these documents he abstracts all useful material for his work and adds it to the fund of material used for his study;
- he assigns missions having to do with his work to liaison officers and general staff officers who he knows will be present at the scene of combat;
- he makes a point of talking with officers visiting the headquarters who have come from units engaged in combat, and with the permission of the chief of staff or the chief of the operations section, he assigns them special tasks to describe aspects of actual combat situations that will contribute to his work;
- at staff and commanders' meetings for critiques of operations that have been completed, he draws up careful minutes (stenographic, when possible) of the proceedings, including all reports, comments, and recommendations that are made;
- he is an active contributor to the army or *front* newspaper, and he also maintains close contact with all military correspondents in his area in order to help and advise them in slanting their reporting toward the most valuable military themes;
- he maintains constant contact and exchange of information with all officers of the command who are engaged in the study of war experience.

10. The senior assistant to the chief of the operations section for the study of war experience arranges and conducts his work in very close cooperation with the chief of the combat training section, the chiefs of the arms and services, the chief of the intelligence section, and the officers of the operations section. He keeps

them informed concerning his work, and points out to them the items that are especially worthy of careful attention in order to round out and make as useful as possible the work that he is doing.

This officer must be exceptionally keen to the situation; he must be inquisitive and resourceful, and must show great perseverance in developing and cultivating sources of information; he must be a hard worker. He must be able to sift facts and arrange them so as to see their significance and be able to generalize from them. He must be able to make correct conclusions from facts, and he must be objective; finally, he must be able to present his conclusions and marshal his evidence in a clear and straightforward manner.

11. Chiefs of staff and chiefs of operations sections must keep in mind that not all officers are ready-made for this type of work. They must give every assistance possible to their assistants for the study of war experience, they must check and critique their work every day, and they must remember that in the beginning it is sufficient that their officers assigned to the study of war experience show good will, work hard, and give evidence that they are able accurately and intelligibly to set forth and organize factual material.

IV. DOCUMENTATION

12. On the basis of analysis of war experience the following types of documents are issued: descriptions of combat actions or of new combat methods, special reports and summaries, outline training exercises for command and staff personnel, directives, instructions, specific orders, reference notes for officers, etc.

    The *front* staff is responsible for the daily dissemination to troops of information derived from combat experience concerning the operational employment of the various arms and services, the employment of the various categories of weapons and equipment, and enemy tactics and techniques.

13. The description of combat and of new combat procedures should follow the general outline set forth below:

    - the situation in which the combat action or new combat procedure occurred;
    - the time and place of the action;
    - enemy forces and nature of enemy opposition;
    - detailed description of the action (or of the way in which the new combat method was applied): who, what, how, against what opposition;
    - detailed descriptions of the results, with indications of demonstrated advantages and disadvantages;
    - conclusions and recommendations.

    All descriptions, reports, summaries, and in general all reports concerning war experience should be accompanied by sketches, photos, diagrams, tables of data, and captured documents, whenever possible.

14. The collection, analysis, generalization, and publication of reports and conclusions concerning war experience should, in general, comply with the following list of general priorities:

    - organization and conduct of *front* and army operations;

- control and direction of *front* and army operations and of combined-arms combat;
- organization of coordination between the arms and services in operations and in combined-arms actions;
- the basic characteristics of infantry combat and of the actions of the arms and services under various climatic, local, and other special conditions;
- methods of forcing rivers, withdrawal, breaking out of encirclement, and pursuit;
- antitank combat methods;
- massed employment and new ways of using tanks, artillery, and air power;
- joint operations of ground troops and fleet units; and of ground troops and naval river flotillas;
- rear services and supply in operations, and the organization of the combat rear area (up through division) and of the operational rear (up through *front*);
- the organization and security of main and reserve CPs, and the methods of staff work at supplementary command and control points;
- the use of radio, and methods of secure signal communications in the exercise of command;
- experience in the large-scale use of engineer obstacles, and in the use of deception.

15. *Front* chiefs of staff will:

- make quarterly reports of progress made in the study of war experience, and of the plan for such study for the ensuing quarter;
- on the 20th of each month render brief reports of the results of current study of war experience, setting forth generalizations arrived at concerning combat methods of the various arms and services, and the combat employment of materiel;
- send by immediate cable any such information of particular importance which may be of significance to the Red Army as a whole;
- forward studies, reports, summaries, etc, for publication in the "Collection of Materials Based on Studies of War Experience".

Chief of the Section for the Application of War
Experience of the General Staff of the Red Army,
Maj General P. Vechny, 6 Nov. 1942

WAR EXPERIENCE

The first volume of war experience analysis was published in August 1942 prior to the issuance of the November order. The volume accurately reflects the problems apparent in the system prior to November 1942. It is a thin volume and it covers experiences only in random fashion. A short introductory section spells out the purposes of the collection process while another article directly addresses why war experiences were being published. A subsequent second volume, published later in 1942, responded more directly to the

November order by including far more comprehensive coverage of major operations in late 1941, in particular the Moscow Operation (December 1941–February 1942).

David M. Glantz
Director of Research
Soviet Army Studies Office

NOTES

1. A. A. Strokov, ed., *Istoriia voennogo iskusstva* [A history of military art] (Moscow: Voenizdat, 1966), pp.323–4.
2. Prior to 1953 the Soviets subdivided the war into four periods by treating 1944 and 1945 as separate periods.
3. S.A. Gladysh, "Obobshchenie i ispol'zovanie boevogo opyta v pervom periode Velikoi Otechestvennoi voiny" [The generalization and use of combat experience in the first period of the Great Patriotic War] *Voenno-istoricheskii zhurnal* [Military-historical journal] No. 7 (July) 1987, 14.
4. Ibid., 15.

GENERAL STAFF OF THE RED ARMY

COLLECTION OF MATERIALS ON THE STUDY OF WAR EXPERIENCE

No. 1

July–August 1942*

VOENNOE IZDATEL'STVO
NARODNOGO KOMISSARIATA
OBORONY SOIUZA SSR
MOSCOW – 1942

*This date refers to the date of publication

The General Staff of the Red Army is publishing collections of materials on the study of war experience.

The purpose of the *Collection* is to bring the experience of combat actions of the Great Patriotic War to the active service troops of the Red Army, reserve organizations, military academies, and command personnel of the main and central directorates of the People's Commissariat of Defense.

As a guide, the *Collection* will include the following material:

- problems of organization and the conduct of operations;
- problems of control of *front* and army operations and combined arms battle;
- organization of joint operation of combat arms in an operation and a combined arms battle;
- fundamentals of infantry battle and activities of combat arms;
- leading instructions on the tactical use of combat arms;
- combat experience of the artillery offensive;
- combat experience of the mass use of aviation;
- methods of the tactical use of tanks;
- methods and devices of antitank defense;
- combat experience of troop activity in winter and under special conditions;
- joint actions of ground forces with the army and sea flotillas;
- theses of combined arms regulations and manuals being reworked according to the experience of the war;
- annotations of materials with a restrictive signature stamp, which have been and are being published by the main and central directorates of the People's Commissariat of Defense.

The *Collection* is a secret document inasmuch as in it is reflected the immediate experience of the active service Red Army, and secret data on the organization and arming of troops are given.

In using and storing the *Collection* it is incumbent to follow the rules and regulations concerning secret documents.

The *Collection* is for regimental commanders of all combat arms.

General Staff of the Red Army

August 1942.

Department for the Use of Combat Experience

CONTENTS

Actions for the Destruction of Large Encircled Enemy Groupings

Actions for encircling and destroying include coordinated strikes on the flanks and rear of the enemy combined with a simultaneous advance from the front.

In the encirclement one should, in the first instance, strive to deprive the enemy of freedom of maneuver and of the possibility of receiving assistance from neighboring units and from the rear.

The success of battles for encirclement depends on the speed and decisiveness of actions and the uninterrupted interaction of all forces involved in the encirclement.

As a rule, the troops implementing the encirclement conduct a battle with an inverted front and require the securing of their flanks and rear from unexpected enemy counterattacks and counterstrikes. This is achieved by both interaction with neighboring formations* and by their own measures for supporting the encircling troops.

---

* Translator's note: the Russian terms *soedinenie* and *ob'edinenie* are usually both translated as "formation", with the American understanding to be a difference in size: *soedinenie* – division, corps, brigade; *ob'edinenie* – army, *front*. The 1986 edition of the *Military Encyclopedia Dictionary* (Moscow: Voenizdat, 1986) gives the following definitions:

– *soedinenie* – a military formation consisting of several units or a number of lower level *soedinenie*, usually of various combat arms (forces), special troops (services), and support and maintenance units (subunits). There are formations of both permanent and temporary organization. The formations are defined as operational, operational-tactical, and tactical, depending on the composition and missions being resolved. The aircraft carrier strike formation in the US Navy is considered an operational formation; army, rifle, mechanized, tank, cavalry, and other corps in the Second World War, and sometimes squadrons of surface ships were considered operational-tactical formations; divisions, brigades, etc. are considered tactical formations;

– *ob'edinenie* – a military formation made up of several *soedinenie* or lower level *ob'edinenie*, as well as units and installations. The *ob'edinenie* may be strategic, operational-strategic, operational, or operational-tactical, depending on the composition and missions being resolved. The *ob'edinenie* may also be territorial combined arms.

For the sake of consistency, throughout this translation, unless otherwise indicated, "formation" will refer to *soedinenie*.

1

On the whole, an operation for encircling and destroying large enemy groupings under modern conditions is a more complex matter than it was in previous wars.

An operation of this type requires exceptional purposefulness, speed, valor, and bravery from the command.

Troops implementing the encirclement should be able to conduct close fighting and battle with an inverted front interacting with infantry weapons, tanks, artillery, and aviation.

In the complex operation for encirclement, most crucial is the concluding stage – the destruction of the encircled enemy grouping. Below are given some conclusions and suggestions concerning the experience of the winter operations of the active service troops of the Red Army in 1942.

The Great Patriotic War gave a number of examples of operations for encircling large enemy forces by troops of the Red Army, in which the stage of destruction of the encircled troops intolerably delayed our further actions (Demiansk grouping of the enemy's 16th Army, Iukhnov enemy grouping, and others).

The reasons why the stage of destruction of the encircled enemy forces was delayed lie in the mistakes of the *front* and army command and their staffs in organizing the operation.

Instead of using its superiority in forces and advantages in its operational position by quickly attacking the encircled enemy with all its forces, breaking him up, and destroying him piecemeal, without being diverted by any other missions, command often dispersed troop efforts: it attempted to accomplish simultaneously other missions without having finished off the encircled enemy. As a result the operations took on a delayed nature with little effect, while the encircled enemy was able to render prolonged resistance and paralyze our further offensive activities.

The encircled enemy troops were able to render prolonged resistance for a number of reasons.

Our forces designated for destroying the encircled enemy were usually deployed equally along the entire front of encirclement and did not have the necessary superiority on the directions from which it would have been necessary to begin to split the grouping.

As a consequence of the delay in destroying the encircled enemy forces, the latter were able to organize a strong, all-round defense.

The slowness of the advance on the chosen primary directions made it possible for the enemy, acting along internal operational lines, to regroup simultaneously and bring up reserves to the threatened sectors.

The presence of strong transport aviation made it possible for the enemy to supply his encircled troops with ammunition, food, and reinforcements, and to evacuate the wounded by air. Thus, in the encircled Demiansk grouping of the German 16th Army, delivery in March by Ju–52 aircraft occurred on a rather large scale (1,088 flights in the first ten days, 778 in the second ten, 1,204 in the third ten). In the course of 20 days in March, 1,431 cargo parachutes were dropped for enemy troops encircled in the area of Kholm.

Stores of ammunition, food and fuel available in areas occupied by encircled enemy troops (Demiansk, Kholm, Sukhinichi) also made the prolonged resistance of the encircled formation possible.

Proceeding from the features of a modern operational defense of large encircled enemy groupings, for their destruction it is incumbent to be guided by the following:

1. Upon completion of the encirclement it is necessary to organize immediately and implement actions directed toward the rout and complete destruction of the encircled enemy forces, without giving him the opportunity to consolidate an all-round defense. These actions basically should come down to simultaneous concentric strikes of the greatest number of available forces from 2–3 directions for the purpose of splitting the enemy grouping into several isolated groups, with their subsequent piecemeal destruction.

2. If the encircled enemy manages to organize a strong all-round defense, the fight against which may be protracted, it is necessary for the army (*front*) command to allot sufficient forces to develop the success on the primary direction of army (*front*) actions, and to create with the reserves and second echelons a grouping, the purpose of which will be the destruction of the encircled enemy. The actions of the troops assigned to destroy the encircled enemy must always be united under a single command.

3. Having completed the encirclement of the enemy and solidly blocked his possible directions of penetration, it is necessary to isolate him immediately from the air. For this, the following are necessary:
    –   to destroy enemy transport aviation both at his primary airfields and at the airfields in the encircled zone; using the *front* and main command air forces, to simultaneously organize and conduct battle for supremacy in the air against enemy combat aviation in the interests of the blockading army;

3

- to create special fighter aviation groups to combat enemy transport aviation on routes, and, by means of patrols and ambushes, to hinder the transport of enemy cargo and personnel;
- to provide for the ground troops of the blockading army, in addition to the antiaircraft means located on the enemy transport aviation routes, special sniper teams armed with automatic weapons on those routes to engage low-flying enemy transport aircraft; in addition, all ground forces of the blockading army must counter enemy aviation (especially transport aviation) using their infantry weapons, including antitank guns.

4. It is necessary to prepare carefully and secretly the operation for destruction of the encircled enemy; the primary aim is to perform the mission quickly and with surprise strikes to prevent the enemy's organizing assistance from without.

5. During the preparatory period it is necessary to do the following in the shortest time:
- conduct reconnaissance boldly, daringly, and uninterruptedly, trying to discover the weak links of the defense; the conduct of reconnaissance must in no way reveal the direction of our prepared strikes; night reconnaissance must be conducted actively and vigilantly to find out promptly the signs and directions of enemy attempts to break out of the encirclement;
- using the broken nature of the front, send into enemy positions small groups of sub-machine gunners and sappers (including airborne) to blow up storage depots and destroy transports and trains; for the same purpose, use long-range artillery and aviation, with broad use of fighter aviation on enemy supply routes ("hunters" on roads);
- conduct particular operations, if the situation makes it expedient, for capturing the most important centers, railroads, dirt roads, and strong points for improving our own initial position and providing communications among groupings of the blockading forces.

6. It is necessary to conduct operations for destroying an encircled enemy decisively and with a total effort of all forces. On the basis of the plan of operation and in accordance with the actual situation, the following are the guiding principles:
- having assembled superior forces on several decisive directions and operating concentrically with them, the enemy should be broken up and destroyed piecemeal; on those directions where dynamic endeavors are not being carried out, the enemy should be reliably contained;

- neither uncoordinated actions of attacking troops nor actions taking place at different times should be allowed;
- actions of our troops on directions leading to a split of the encircled enemy grouping must be supported by mass aviation and tank strikes;
- the maneuver of enemy reserves within the encircled area (by aviation, assaults [*desant*], and sub-machine gun groups) must be prevented, simultaneously with the attack from the front;
- on directions of probable attempts to break out of the encirclement there should be reserves – ambushes to destroy enemy units which have broken out of the encirclement.

7. Support of actions of the blockading forces on the side of the primary front of fighting against the enemy is assigned to the higher command (army, *front*). Some of the troops implementing the encirclement will usually conduct a battle against an inverted front; therefore, the command of the encircling group must take all measures for continual readiness to repel possible enemy attacks from the rear.

8. The success of the encirclement operation, for the most part, depends on uninterrupted interaction of all forces involved in the encirclement and on skillful combination of fire and maneuver. Therefore, unparalleled attention must be given to problems of organizing control in encirclement operations.

   In view of the extent of the front of encircling troops, the commander of the army or operational group cannot be limited to control of only his own command position; in addition to the command post a further 2–3 auxiliary command posts should be organized, where specially assigned staff commanders with the necessary means of communications and movement collect data about the situation, report the information to their staff, and transmit orders received from their headquarters to the troops.

   The basic means of control in an encirclement operation will be radio communications. Widely deployed radio networks should be used in complete accordance with the order of the Headquarters of the Supreme Commander-in-Chief dated 30 May 1942, No. 00107.

Some Conclusions on Assault ("Desant") Operations During 1941

In the overall course of the fierce struggle against the German invaders, the first year of the Great Patriotic War, on all our coastal theaters of strategic military operations, is characterized by the broad use of assault (*desant*) operations.

The large number of assault operations is explained by the fact that by their nature they are the most active form of interaction of the Red Army and Navy, and, therefore, make it possible to use most effectively the combat means of the Red Army and Navy and facilitate the fight of ground forces on coastal sectors of the front. Assault operations represent one of the tightest forms of joint operation of the Red Army and Navy in achieving a single goal – the rout of the enemy.

The practical experience of the first year of the war gave positive models of well-prepared and well-executed assault operations. However, in the conclusions given below concerning assault operations of 1941, emphasis is given to reasons which resulted in flaws in the joint operations of ground forces with the Navy.

The study of fundamental mistakes by combined arms and naval commanders helps to find reliable means of eliminating them in future fighting against the German invaders.

A review of assault operations of ground forces and the Navy carried out in 1941 shows that, together with the well-prepared and well-executed operations, some were carried out with a breach of the requirements of regulations and manuals, often leading to unnecessary sacrifices.

The primary flaws in conducting assault operations were the following:

1. Assault forces were numerically small and weakly armed, as a consequence of which the forces and means did not always correspond to the assigned missions.

2. Assault forces were not specially prepared for night operations, operations in a forest, or in populated areas; they were also often sent on an operation without preparation for conducting battle under conditions of an amphibious landing.
3. There was an absence of close cooperation of the disembarked assault forces with units of the Red Army; the majority of assaults were not supported by an advance of ground forces from the front, which was also one of the primary reasons for the lack of success of some assaults.
4. Poor support of the disembarkation and landing actions ashore by combat aviation resulted in unnecessary losses of personnel and transport.
5. Poor support, or complete lack of support, by ship artillery fire led to assault forces being left to their own devices after disembarkation.
6. There was insufficient reconnaissance of the landing areas and enemy fire means and personnel, as well as weak interaction of naval reconnaissance with air and ground reconnaissance of the air and ground forces.
7. Unsatisfactory work of the combined arms and naval staffs resulted in great inadequacies in command and control during the assault operations.
8. The organization and work of communications in a number of instances did not provide for interaction between the disembarked forces and the ground forces units, support ships, and aviation.
9. Inadequate hydrographic support of the crossing and disembarkation area for the landing led to ships running aground, damages, delays, and sometimes a foiling of the assault operations.
10. The narrow front for the majority of disembarkations made it possible for the enemy to determine with sufficient ease the primary direction of the strike, quickly bring up forces to the landing area, and organize countermeasures.
11. Inadequately dynamic and bold actions of the assault forces ashore made it possible for the enemy to take the initiative.
12. There was insufficient knowledge of enemy tactics and poor study of the experience of earlier assaults.

A more detailed examination of the enumerated flaws leads to the following conclusions:

COMPOSITION OF ASSAULT FORCES AND MEANS

The field manual states that "the force and means of an assault depend on the mission assigned to it." Consequently, the composition of the assault force and its fire power should be such that the assault can fulfill its primary mission ashore and achieve the indicated goal. In fact, as a rule, assaults were small in numbers (company, battalion) and were inadequately armed, without antitank means or mortars. In the majority of cases neither the numerical composition nor the arms were suitable for the assigned missions. Assaults were small in numbers while the missions were great. This lack of correspondence was felt especially sharply in the assaults on the Leningrad Front.

Thus, the assaults on 23 and 25 September 1941 in the consolidated enemy area east of Schluesselburg consisted of 229 men, i.e., essentially a reinforced rifle company, and had the mission of capturing Schluesselburg and subsequently advancing in a southeast direction to join up with our units east of Siniavino.

The number of troops which disembarked was clearly inadequate, especially as the landing took place on a reinforced coastal sector occupied by the enemy.

The disembarkations in the area of Strel'na are a similar example; in addition, here can be noted instances of assigning missions which were not completely correct or clear. Thus, the forces which disembarked on 6 and 8 October had the mission of "joining up with a battalion which landed earlier and then joining up with army units." Neither the naval command nor the command of the forces which disembarked knew where the battalion which had landed earlier was located or what its situation was.

PREPARATION OF ASSAULT FORCES

In the majority of cases the assault forces did not have preliminary training in fighting under conditions similar to those they would have to face; as a result, they poorly oriented themselves ashore and acted unskillfully and indecisively, giving the enemy the opportunity to bring up its own forces to the landing area or to withdraw unnoticed and without losses.

Thus, as a result of the absence of adequate reconnaissance and dynamic operations of the forces which disembarked in the area of Kerch', the enemy, under threat of being cut off by the assault forces which had disembarked earlier in Feodosiia, managed to leave Kerch', and the evacuation was only discovered the next day by the units of the Kerch' assault operation.

The assault forces included units of the Red Army and Navy. Both these and others were usually not prepared for fulfilling their assigned missions. Here the weak preparation of assaults made up of navy personnel should be especially noted; they lacked not only preparation for operating under conditions specific for assault forces, but also any preparation in general for conducting land battle.

Naval infantry units, as a rule, were thrown into the operation immediately after their establishment or they were formed in the course of the operation. Thus, the noted qualities of sailors – heroism, bravery, and devotion to the motherland – were not supplemented by the ability to fight on dry land.

In preparing the assault operations, ground forces and naval command underestimated the significance of training troops to conduct battle under assault conditions and did not allot the necessary time for training.

One can also speak about the special naval training of assault forces: embarking on ships, loading materiel, transferring to landing means, and disembarking. The fundamental reason for the lack of preparation of troops was too short a time given to the ground forces command for completing the assault operation. In the majority of cases the short time was explained by the attempt to maintain the secrecy and surprise of the landing with respect to the enemy.

In reality secrecy and surprise were achieved and the assault forces disembarked either without losses or with insignificant losses; but after disembarkation the forces found themselves in an extremely difficult situation as a consequence of the lack of knowledge of the system of the enemy defense, and in the majority of cases they did not fulfill their missions.

With only a short time for preparation of troops and support, it was impossible to organize any satisfactory reconnaissance. For this reason they were also not able to organize interaction, not only of the army with the navy and air force, but also within the assault forces.

The lack of time for preparing troops and the operation itself were the primary reasons for a portion of the assault forces not coping with their assigned missions.

Where time was allotted for preliminary preparation the results were completely different. The disembarkation of the forces at Feodosiia can serve as an example of this. Here the preparation of the troops continued for more than half a month, and, in spite of some units being replaced

9

by others before the operation itself, the embarkation, disembarkation, and troop action ashore, nevertheless, proceeded rapidly and in an organized manner. Basic data about the enemy were obtained by a net of agents and by operational intelligence. Navigational equipping of the approaches was provided beforehand by setting up light buoys and by placing submarines and launches with fires at the positions.

In spite of the forces being landed in a strongly fortified enemy area, their actions were bold, sure, and decisive. The first wave of the assault in Feodosiia proved itself excellently; it not only captured the pier, but also boldly moved into the town and seized part of it before the disembarkation of the first and subsequent echelons of the assault, without allowing the enemy to collect himself.

INTERACTION OF TROOPS

The organization of interaction, both within the assault and with units of the Red Army, aviation, and the navy, had many shortcomings.

The disembarkation sometimes took place without considering the possibility of support of the assault operations by the advance of Red Army units from the front; in some instances the units of the Red Army in general did not know about the forces which had disembarked.

The landings in the area of Schluesselburg, Strel'na, and N. Petergof, coordinated with interacting armies and actions of ground forces units, were not supported; the fighting was isolated and success could not be achieved. The situation was further aggravated by the fact that from the moment of disembarkation, communications with assault units ceased; neither the army nor the navy knew about the actions of the units ashore, or their situation.

AVIATION SUPPORT OF ASSAULTS

The majority of assault operations were carried out in the complete absence of combat aviation support. In the best case a rather limited aviation force assigned for support was unable to fulfill its mission.

There was also no tactical interaction of aviation with the disembarked assault units. As a rule aviation operated against indicated positions of presumed location of enemy troops and fire points. Aviation did not know where the assault forces were, what they were doing, whether or not they should bomb this point, or if it was necessary to bomb another.

In the majority of instances there was no cover of the landing area by fighter aviation, as a result of which the landings suffered losses in personnel and craft.

The troops had no practical experience in joint operations of amphibious and airborne assaults.

The assaults of the Northern and Black Sea Fleets in capturing the Finnish islands can serve as an example of good interaction of aviation with an assault. The embarkation, crossing, and disembarkation were covered by fighter aviation, and bomber aviation delivered strikes against enemy fire positions and personnel during the approach and the disembarkation.

SUPPORT OF A DISEMBARKED ASSAULT FORCE BY NAVAL SHIPS

The landings of the Northern Fleet and the Black Sea Fleet in Feodosiia are positive examples of well-organized interaction. In these instances communications of the assault forces with the ships and of the ships with the staff of the interacting army operated uninterruptedly. Together with the assault of the first wave, surveillance posts from supporting assaults of ships with reliable means of communication (radio, telephone, rockets, flags, semaphores) were disembarked. A special ship having radio and visual communications with the support ships and telephone communications with the ships, the assault commander, and the surveillance posts, stood at the disembarkation area.

Such a communications ship had the mission of supporting by means of communications the detachment of support ships with surveillance posts and the commander of the assault troops in case of a breakdown in the radio equipment of the latter. Ship firing was conducted upon the requisition and target indication of the assault commander and was corrected by the posts which disembarked ashore.

In addition, a communications officer from the headquarters of the interacting army was assigned for communications and mutual information with ground forces units, and orientation on the terrain of the assault command. The landing was covered from the air by fighter aviation. As a result of good interaction, the assault forces disembarked almost without losses and operated on dry land assuredly and rapidly.

In all other cases of disembarking forces, the role of the navy and flotillas basically was transporting and landing the troops ashore.

There was no artillery support for the majority of landings. After the landing the ships either left altogether or conducted fire at their own

11

discretion, without target indication on the part of the commander of the assault troops and without correction. Those firing did not know to what extent their action helped or hindered the assault operations.

Surveillance posts did not disembark ashore with the landing forces, and there was no communication with the landing forces; therefore, there could be no requisitions or target indications from the assault commander for artillery support.

RECONNAISSANCE

Interaction of forces and means of naval, army, and air force reconnaissance were weak. Reconnaissance operated passively: there was no systematic reconnaissance of the forward edge and depth of the enemy defense in disembarkation areas and regions, nor was there a study of the tactical devices and technical means of the enemy. As a rule reconnaissance of the landing areas by special groups from submarines, launches, and aircraft, taking of prisoners, interrogation of the local population, aerial photographs, diversionary reconnaissance operations, disinformation, use of radio, light, and sound reconnaissance were not carried out, with the exception of individual cases.

The assault forces disembarked blindly; they did not know what awaited them ashore or against what kinds of forces they would have to fight. The lack of knowledge of the enemy's fire means positions often led to the foiling of the operation, an incomplete assault, or the necessity of finding a new disembarkation area.

Thus, because of strong enemy fire the disembarkation of forces in the area of Schluesselburg on 26 September 1941 was called off. For the same reason the landing in the area of Strel'na on 8 October 1941 was not completely disembarked; the assault forces on the northern coast of the Kerch' Peninsula in December 1941 were forced to find a new disembarkation area and were partially returned to base.

There were instances where the available data on enemy fire means were disregarded and support measures were not taken.

COMMUNICATIONS OPERATIONS

As a consequence of inadequate training of radio operators, poor functioning of or damage to equipment, in the majority of cases there were no radio communications for assault groups during the disembarkation and in the battle.

Where experienced naval radio operators or ship radio stations were attached to the assault forces, or where a special communications ship (at the disembarkation area) was assigned, communications operated well and the situation in the landing area on land was known to both naval and army commands.

The experience of assault operations showed the possibility of wide use for communications: rockets, tracer bullets and shells, continual and flashing fire, and other means.

At the same time the inability of the communications men to combat enemy interference and organize a rapid transfer from one type of communications to another was manifested.

In preparing for the assault operations many unnecessary demasking (*demaskirovka*) telephone, telegraph, and radio conversations took place. There was little personal contact.

WORK OF COMMAND AND STAFFS

Staffs did not always provide commanders with the data and operational-tactical calculations necessary for decision-making.

The formulation of documents at headquarters took up too much time; consequently part of the landing operation was carried out in a disorderly formation (*poriadok*).

Staff control of the participants' correct understanding of their role in the operation and the mission, and prevention of mistakes and conflicts in command of the assault operation were not always implemented.

Reasons for the poor work of the combined arms and naval command and staffs can be seen in the following:

Combined arms commanders and staffs are poorly acquainted with the tactical-technical properties of the Navy; they have a poor concept of the essence of joint work with the naval staff in planning an assault operation; they are not able to organize control from auxiliary positions, which have been provided with radios and mobile means of communication; they formally work out issues of interaction in numerous documents, but in the actual execution of an assault operation they cannot quickly re-establish interaction which has been lost.

The combined arms command did not always clearly and correctly present the missions to the assault forces, and often changed them, as happened in carrying out the assault operation on the northern coast of the Kerch' Peninsula. In this operation the decisions concerning the composition of the assault forces and the areas of operation were changed three times, resulting in the assault forces' not knowing their missions in the new disembarkation areas; the actions of the assault forces ashore and of the ships during disembarkation were indecisive and lacked skill.

The naval command and staffs worked more accurately, but, to a significant degree, the inadequacies mentioned above were characteristic of them as well.

A typical shortcoming in the work of the cooperating commanders and staffs was the fact that the nature of the assault operation under modern conditions had not been made clear and was mastered with difficulty. In formally following the instructions of regulations and manuals of the Red Army and Navy, the command and staffs insufficiently considered such elements as the obstinacy of the enemy in the defense, the enemy's mass use of mortar and automatic weapons fire, powerful bomb strikes, and assault activity in the areas of disembarkation.

In the actions of their troops the element of preliminary and very careful preparation of the assault units was not given sufficient consideration.

STUDY OF THE EXPERIENCE OF ASSAULT OPERATIONS

The experience of the first assault operations was poorly studied; consequently subsequent disembarkations took place without taking into account either the shortcomings which had occurred or enemy tactics. Only this would explain, for example, the disembarkation of four successive small units in the area of Strel'na at a time when enemy tactics did not change.

The forces disembarked almost without resistance, but as soon as they were ashore the enemy opened strong rifle-machine gun and artillery-mortar fire against the landing area; the assault forces were cut off from the water and the ships supporting them; communications ceased and all attempts to reestablish them, to land reinforcements, or to deliver ammunition were repelled by strong fire. Under these conditions a small and isolated assault force, in the majority of cases, was not able to carry out its missions.

MEANS OF TRANSPORTING AND DISEMBARKING ASSAULT FORCES

The experience of assault operations which have been carried out demonstrates the following:

- the necessity of having small, rapid landing ships with light armored protection of personnel and mechanisms against bullets and fragments;
- the inexpediency of using vessels for landing which are not self-propelled;
- the possibility of the broad use of combat ships of all classes for the transport and disembarkation of forces ashore;
- the excellent qualities of basic types of launches and motorboats, which make them not only ideal for landing and direct fire support, but also good for transport of assault forces short distances.

The transport of assault forces on combat ships demonstrates the following advantages:

1. The great speed of combat ships makes it possible during darkness to transport assault forces great distances unnoticed by the enemy, and to disembark them in areas where the enemy least expects them.
2. The overall number of transport vessels of an assault detachment is reduced, as is its vulnerability to enemy aviation and submarines; control is facilitated.
3. The creation of a special detachment for protection of the ships is not required, since the protection missions can be fulfilled by the landing ships themselves.
4. The destruction of fire points at the moment of landing and artillery support of the assault forces ashore can also be implemented by these ships independently.
5. Thanks to their great speed and artillery weapons, combat ships can, in suppressing enemy fire on the march, penetrate harbors and disembark assault forces directly on wharves and jetties, as was done in Feodosiia on 29 December 1941.

CONCLUSIONS

Concrete proposals for eliminating shortcomings which have shown up in assault operations by the combat experience of the first year of the Great Patriotic War can be summarized by the following:

1. It is necessary to collect and carefully study all the accumulated experience of assault operations which have been carried out.
2. In carrying out the operation all command personnel must acquire knowledge of and fulfill regulation requirements. It must be taken into account that in the new plan of the *Field Regulations* and the *Manual for*

Joint Operations of Ground Forces and the Navy and Naval Flotillas, which is being developed, the experience of previous assault operations has been considered.

3. The composition of the assault forces, the means attached to them, and their weapons should meet the requirements which arise from the nature of the mission assigned to them and the operational situation of the area of activity.

4. Special attention must be given to the preparation of assault forces and all command personnel for executing the operation. Each commander should clearly envision his role and place in the overall course of the operation, foresee all variations of the situation, which may become complicated for him in the process of carrying out the operation, and be aware of the conditions under which his unit (subunit) must operate and for which actions it must be prepared. Taking into consideration all these data, the commander is obliged to prepare his unit for assured, bold, and decisive actions.

It should also be remembered that landing actions during the approach to the shore and in battle on the shore usually begin as a whole series of independent combat actions unconnected regarding location, and performed by individual groups of troops which have landed; this gradually develops into a combined arms battle.

Such a battle development makes high demands on everyone, including young commanders, with respect to bravery, decisiveness, and independence of action, especially at the commencement of the landing.

5. In planning an operation it is absolutely necessary to provide the required time for its preparation and for the preparation of the assault forces. Here it is necessary to consider that the insufficiency of time for the preparation of the operation reduces the quality of reconnaissance and organization of assault forces and means, and the quality of preparation of troops; it inevitably leads to uncertain actions in a complex situation.

The observation of secrecy during the preparation for an operation should mainly proceed by a reduction of unnecessary telephone, telegraph, and radio communications.

6. The disembarkation of any units must be in strict accordance with the actions of the ground forces on the primary front of the coastal sector. It is particularly important to keep this in mind during the actual execution of the operation, when the nature of the indicated actions on the primary front of the ground forces and the time for their execution

often predetermine the success of the actions of the assault forces and the success of front actions on the whole.

7. The assault forces should have reliable cover from the air and maximally use their own air defense means at all stages of the operation (embarkation, crossing, and landing). Aviation allotted for support should be prepared for tactical interaction with the assault forces ashore; here special attention should be given to the method and means of mutual recognition of ground troops and their combat aviation.

8. In assigning missions to the navy (flotilla) for an assault operation, special attention should be given to problems in the organization of interaction of naval ships with the actions of the assault forces ashore. Reliable duplication of communications facilities of the assault commander with the ship formation supporting him, and the correction of ship artillery fire from the shore are obligatory conditions for providing this interaction.

It should be kept in mind that the unit which is landing can at first only count on the support of individual guns being put into operation by the infantry. Therefore, it is necessary to use ship artillery for landing cover or dive bombers and fighter aviation at the appearance of an enemy target at the shore line, the latter to compensate for artillery fire immediately before and during the landing. Here the airplanes making the last raid indicate to the troops by means of a special signal the cessation of bombardment, so that the units can more quickly take advantage of the bombardment. Setting up smoke screens from the aircraft may also be advantageous.

9. The staff organizing the assault operation is obliged to provide appropriate data and operational-tactical calculations to the commanders making the decision; organize and use all reconnaissance forces and means of the army, air forces, and navy; formulate documents and promptly give them to those involved; verify if the participants in the operation correctly understand the missions; control the execution of the command decisions during the operation itself.

10. The staff organizing the assault operation and the commander of the assault forces must have all necessary data about the enemy before embarkation begins. The assault forces should know whom they may encounter while carrying out their mission.

The assault detachment should know the situation at sea and on land, and with whom it will come into contact near the shore and on the landing sector, including the most immediate areas. The detachment should know the mission standing before it, and be prepared, with respect to personnel and equipment, to carry it out.

The detachment should have at its disposal a sufficient number of good maps, aerial photographs (large-scale and recent, with an indication of vegetation located on the terrain) and oblique photos of the coastal area, which facilitates preparation and orientation for the assault forces' future actions.

It is difficult to establish beforehand in what area the landing of individual subunits will actually take place; therefore, the unit must be equipped with maps and photographs of a large section of the coastal area.

11. It is very important for the assault force commander to find out at which points and to what extent the landing operation succeeded; therefore, a system of recognition signals between ground troops, air forces and naval ships should be developed.

The assault units should have instruments for visual and pyrotechnical signalization (signal flags, signalling panels, rockets, etc.).

12. If the disembarkation takes place in an echeloned manner (and this will occur most often), then the commanders of the first combat echelon should know if and when they can count on the arrival of the second combat echelon forces in the area of their actions.

In supplying the first combat echelon with ammunition and provisions, it should be taken into account that a unit which has landed will be left to its own devices for a prolonged period, and, with the changing situation, will be forced to manage with only the ammunition it brought along. This circumstance requires that the unit be sufficiently equipped; it is particularly important to have a significant quantity of ammunition necessary for the fire cover of the landing. As a rule, ammunition should be loaded and unloaded on all crossing ships, together with weapons. Instruments which are water-sensitive and ammunition should be packed in watertight packing.

Small storage depots are built in the coastal zone for the unloaded goods, as the advancing units do not take them along.

The commander of the subunit or unit which has landed should know what quantity of ammunition he has at his disposal, since this can have a great influence on decisions made by him during the battle.

13. Landing on a wide front is the best means for suppressing flanking fire, which prevents the disembarkation of the forces afloat or in an open coastal zone. In the course of the first hours of the battle for the shore, the defending side, which is being attacked on a wide front, will also have

to conduct the battle with its own forces only, which are dispersed over a large area; they will probably be able to get reinforcements from reserves only at some points.

14. A unit which has landed, after capturing the nearest sector of the landing bridgehead, will be able to conduct battle reconnaissance solely with its own means. Therefore, both for the unit itself and for the leadership, it is important to discover enemy countermeasures early. Air reconnaissance should carry out this urgent mission.

The results of reconnaissance should be transmitted to the units fighting ashore by dropping reports directly on the position of the unit or by reporting on radio; otherwise they will arrive too late.

Command positions ashore should be quickly indicated by laying out an air signal post sign.

The number of successfully executed landings, including large ones under complex conditions (Feodosiia) indicates that units of the Red Army and Navy are capable of executing any assault operations under any conditions; however, this requires well thought-out preparation of the operations in all respects; correct organization and deployment of forces and means; careful study of enemy tactics, forces, and means; and bold and decisive actions of all operation participants in carrying out the assigned missions.

A Brief Review of the Tactical Use of Antitank Defense Assets

In the course of the Great Patriotic War the Red Army accumulated rich experience in fighting against tanks.

Our troops now have at their disposal various means, in the form of powerful artillery, antitank guns, flame-thrower–incendiary means, antitank hand grenades, and various engineer means, for fighting against enemy tanks.

Below are given brief conclusions on the tactical use of each of these means and the fundamental instructions for organizing an antitank defense according to the experience of the Great Patriotic War.

I. ARTILLERY

Artillery of all types is the primary fire means for destroying tanks and repelling mass tank attacks. The experience of the late battles, especially on the Khar'kov Axis, attests to this; here our artillery from 14 to 16 May 1942 conducted a fierce battle against strong enemy tank groups and successfully repelled their attack. This battle demonstrated that prepared, persistent, and well-controlled troops would always be able to repel a mass tank attack.

In the above-mentioned battle our artillerymen, in destroying enemy tanks with a high degree of bravery and stubbornness, demonstrated first-class shooting and repelled the many attacks of the 3d and 23d German Tank Divisions, which had gone over to a counteroffensive to re-establish their position. The Germans assembled no fewer than 400 mainly mid-size tanks with motorized infantry and, having gone over to the offensive, counted on success; however, they themselves were routed.

The artillery of the 13th Guards and 244th Rifle Divisions took on the entire weight of the main tank strike. The artillery of the 13th Guards Rifle Division (71 guns), in particular the first battery of the 32d Guards Artillery Regiment, which destroyed 18 tanks, took on the strike of the first tank echelon (consisting of 40 tanks) and of the second tank echelon (consisting of 60 tanks). The second group, consisting of 150 tanks, went over to the attack from another direction against the fire positions of the 244th Rifle Division artillery (66 guns) from 3 directions; firing from the tanks was conducted using armor-piercing and thermite shells. Artillery personnel whose clothes were burning extinguished fire by using dirt and continued to fire against the tanks. In the course of the two-day battles the artillery of the 13th Guards Rifle Division destroyed 50 tanks, and the artillery of the 244th Rifle Division 93 tanks. At the fire positions were antitank guns which, interacting with artillery, repelled the tank attack and damaged 12 enemy tanks.

The Germans organized the tank attack in 3 echelons on the sector of the 244th Rifle Division. Each echelon had 40–45 tanks structured linearly, with intervals of 40–50 meters between tanks. The tank echelons were located at a distance of 200–400 meters from one another and arrived at the initial position in such a formation.

Before the attack the enemy aircraft-corrector let down a green rocket; the tanks answered with a red rocket upward, after which the first tank echelon began to move with a speed of 10–15 kilometers per hour. The first tank echelon stopped before coming within 700–800 meters of the area of the fire positions and began to fire from guns, machine guns, and automatic weapons. At this time the second tank echelon occupied the position of the first, and the third occupied the position of the second. The sub-machine gunners advanced behind the third echelon tanks on armored personnel carriers; in the tanks themselves there were also 1–2 sub-machine gunners who exited from the lower hatches of the tanks.

The tank attacks against the batteries were conducted from 3 directions (pincer movement) from a distance of 500–600 meters.

As a result of this battle, the following was established:

- the most vulnerable areas of the tanks are the tracks and suspension, and the side and rear walls;
- the tank turret breaks away as a result of a direct hit from a 76mm or larger caliber shell;
- all tanks are penetrated by armor-piercing shells; only the side of the tank is penetrated by high explosive (fougasse) grenades;
- use of percussion tube shrapnel is not effective, even if the firing is conducted at a distance of 200 meters or closer.

In using artillery for antitank defense, it is necessary to do the following:

1. Construct an antitank defense on directions favorable for tanks by creating antitank strong points reliably covered by natural and artificial antitank obstacles; individual pieces of ordnance carrying out direct fire, and antitank guns should comprise the basis of the fire system of the antitank strong points.

2. Have all regimental artillery, both antitank and 76mm caliber, at antitank strong points located at the position of the main resistance (the first battle echelons of the regiments); echelon the division artillery and reinforcement artillery in the depth of the defense and arrange it at the antitank strong points for the purpose of destroying enemy tanks which have penetrated.

3. Arrange, in anticipation of a mass tank attack, the field gun batteries of division artillery and part of the reinforcement artillery by guns, including them in the system of antitank strong points; arrange the remaining division and reinforcement artillery at indirect positions on probable directions of movement of enemy tanks; outfit fire positions as antitank positions and cover them without fail with engineer barriers, having a direct field of fire of 800–1,000 meters for howitzers, and 1,000–1,500 meters for guns; outfit antiaircraft artillery positions in the same order.

4. Have all batteries ready to meet attacking enemy tanks with direct fire from primary positions or from positions specially chosen for this purpose; have a constant reserve of armor-piercing shells for the batteries.

5. In all cases attempt to fire against tanks according to norms or close to them; as a rule, fire with armor-piercing shells; in the absence of armor-piercing shells, use grenades with high explosive fuse settings; in firing at a range of up to 400 meters, it is better to aim the gun at the highest visible vertical surface of the tank; at a range greater than 400 meters, aim at the center of the forward, lateral, or rear part of the tank; in firing at the tracks and suspension of the tank, fire from forward and behind – "obliquely" along the driving and driven wheels – is considered most advantageous.

II. ANTITANK GUNS

An antitank gun in the hands of a brave, composed soldier is a reliable weapon which has proved itself in fighting against enemy tanks at close quarters.

Thanks to its weight and dimensions, the gun is a fine, mobile antitank weapon both on the defense and offense.

On one of the sectors of the Southwestern Front, soldiers of the 32d Artillery Regiment destroyed 12 German tanks in 2 days with antitank guns.

On one sector of another front, 14 German tanks attacked along a narrow defile position of our antitank gun platoon (9 guns). Firing at the forward part of the tanks, even from a distance of 250 meters, provided no results, and the tanks continued to move. The outcome of the battle was decided by fire from guns against the tanks' sides. Having lost six tanks, the Germans withdrew in disorder.

The experience of using antitank guns shows that the most vulnerable parts of an enemy tank are its side and rear area, where the motor and fuel tanks are located, and the turret, along the inner surface of which ammunition is located. An armor-piercing/incendiary bullet from an antitank gun pierces the tank armor and breaks off fragments from its inner side. Armor and bullet fragments strike the crew, and the tank catches fire from direct hits of bullets in the motor and fuel tanks.

For the successful use of antitank guns in the overall system of antitank defense, it is necessary to do the following:

1. Use antitank guns in the defense as part of a company/platoon on directions favorable for tanks, so as not to allow their equal distribution along the entire front of the unit; echelon the antitank gun subunits in the depth, and always have a reserve of these weapons to reinforce directions which are favorable for tanks and to repel an attack of enemy tanks from a new direction; in the system of antitank defense of the unit, coordinate the fire of antitank guns with artillery fire and the system of engineer obstacles.

2. Choose the fire positions of the antitank gun groups and subunits, taking into consideration the possibility of conducting flank fire against enemy tanks from a distance of 400 meters up to point blank firing; carefully camouflage the positions and have trenches (slit trenches) for the guns and teams; choose positions behind antitank obstacles, so as to strike the enemy tanks as they tackle the obstacles (in these cases there is often an opportunity to strike the hull floor of the tank); have, in addition to the primary antitank gun fire positions, two–three reserve positions which make it possible to conduct group (three–four guns) directed fire from them with an all-round field of fire; after repelling the tank attack, change without fail the positions of the antitank guns.

23

3. Use antitank guns on the offensive on directions of probable enemy tank counterattack, the guns being directly in the battle formation* of the advancing infantry, echeloned in the depth; with consolidation on captured lines and with a fight within the enemy defense, use the antitank gun subunits to repel counterattacking tanks and to destroy enemy tank ambushes.

III. FLAME-THROWING/INCENDIARY MEANS

The experience of using flame-throwing/incendiary means demonstrates their high degree of effectiveness in fighting against tanks.

On the Volkhov Front, during an enemy tank attack on 15–17 March 1942, 8 enemy tanks were burned and destroyed by the detonation of 65 static flame throwers, together with antitank defense guns.

On the Western Front, from 13 to 29 October 1941 25 enemy tanks and 11 motor vehicles were burned by units of one division using Molotov cocktails.

On the Leningrad Front, on 2 July 1941, subunits of a rifle battalion destroyed 29 enemy tanks and 13 motor vehicles with ammunition by the combined use of hand grenades and Molotov cocktails.

On one sector of the Western Front, fields of Molotov cocktails, on which 3 enemy tanks and 2 motor vehicles burned, were created in the overall system of engineer obstacles. In addition, these fields caused tanks to stop; this was effectively used by tank destroyers which, in their turn, destroyed an additional 17 enemy tanks using Molotov cocktails.

Fire barriers, capable of blocking tank paths and paths of enemy infantry advancing behind them, are also an effective defensive means. On the Western Front in the first days of December 1941, on the path of the probable tank attack a fire barrier 500–550 meters in length was constructed out of combustible materials. With the approach of enemy tanks, the barrier was ignited by static flame throwers and burned for four hours. Upon encountering the burning barrier, the enemy tanks deployed and began to move along it, putting their most vulnerable side under fire of antitank guns. In attempting to go around the fire barrier, some tanks were stopped by the mine and Molotov cocktail fields, which were arranged on the barrier flanks. As a result of the joint actions of the flame-throwing/incendiary means and artillery, 25 of 40 enemy tanks were destroyed. The enemy advance on this sector was frustrated.

*Translator's note: the Russian term *boevoi poriadok* will be translated throughout the document as "battle formation".

The above examples show that fire barriers, when used capably, are an effective means in the fight against enemy tanks.

In using flame-throwing/incendiary means in the fight against enemy tanks, it is necessary to do the following:

1. Arrange defense fire positions of static flame-thrower companies on directions of probable enemy tank advance; choose camouflaged fire positions, entrench and cover the infantry well from enemy reconnaissance; have three–five static flame throwers per battery and echelon them in the depth; fix their positions to tank-proof areas and engineer and fire-incendiary barriers (Molotov cocktail fields, fire barriers, etc.); cover by fire from antitank means all fire positions for static flame-throwers and flame-thrower/incendiary barriers (here it is necessary to carefully organize their interaction with artillery, antitank guns, and tanks); combine the fire barriers with engineer barriers and mine fields; allow enemy tanks to approach to a minimally short distance and burn them by artillery and antitank gun fire.

2. On the offensive broadly use flame-thrower/incendiary means to reinforce lines and objectives captured from the enemy; set up flame-throwers on directions of probable enemy tank counterattack in approximately the same way as indicated above for the defense.

IV. ENGINEER MEANS

Engineer means of antitank defense include the following: ditches, escarpments, traps, barriers, etc.; they were also used against German tanks, especially on defensive lines prepared in advance.

The primary conditions for their successful use are the careful use of terrain and camouflage; these obstacles must definitely be mined and covered by artillery, machine gun, and mortar fire. Otherwise they turn into cover for enemy infantry and, sometimes, tanks.

These obstacles are labor-consuming, and they should therefore be placed, in the first order, on the most probable directions of tank movement.

Under the maneuver-type conditions of the summer operations of the current year, antitank mine fields must be acknowledged as the most dynamic and easily implemented type of engineer obstacle.

Mines should be arranged in antitank mine fields so that any tank path will directly intersect one or two mines. The mines should be carefully camouflaged, and the mine fields should be adapted to the terrain.

For the defense of antitank mine fields, anti-personnel mines should be set up on the approaches to the mine field at 20–100 meters, and in the mine field itself.

All variants of setting up mine fields should be a puzzle to the enemy; for this it is necessary to set up antitank mines in combination with anti-personnel mines, and to widely use guided and dummy mines, mines with anti-lift devices, and booby traps.

The fundamental quality of this type of obstacle is maneuverability, i.e., rapidity in transporting and setting up the mines; this quality is necessary not only in the defense, but also on the offensive (when consolidating on captured lines).

The commanders of formations must have mobile antitank reserves (tanks, antitank guns, antitank rifle subunits, sappers) for an antitank maneuver; they must also have mobile sapper groups with mines and other means of engineer obstacles.

The strength of the antitank defense of the Red Army is in the competent combination of artillery fire, antitank rifle fire, and engineer and flame-throwing/incendiary means.

The main role in the system of antitank defense belongs to artillery, but its fire positions must always be defended by mines and other antitank defense means.

Use of Troop Assets in the Struggle against Enemy Aviation

The experience of the Great Patriotic War has shown that a successful conduct of the struggle against enemy aircraft which are attacking infantry is possible not only using special air defense means (fighter aviation, antiaircraft artillery, antiaircraft machine guns), but also by using fire means which are directly available to the infantry itself.

Small-arms fire has found wide use in the struggle against enemy aircraft. A number of units and formations of the Red Army fighting on the fronts of the Great Patriotic War, thanks to the well-organized and capable use of small-arms fire against air targets, claim more than a dozen enemy aircraft brought down. In April and May 1942 alone, 72 enemy aircraft were brought down by small-arms fire of Red Army field units. In this period on the Kalinin Front alone, 27 aircraft were brought down, and in one army operating on the strike directions, 20 aircraft were brought down in April, comprising 50 per cent of the overall number of enemy aircraft brought down in the zone of the army for this period.

Lately, for the purpose of searching out additional means for the struggle against enemy aircraft, especially against dive bombers, antitank rifles and 76mm guns were used on several fronts. As a result, three aircraft were brought down by antitank rifles and several aircraft were brought down by 76mm guns over a short period of time; in all cases of firing from 76mm guns against aircraft, using shrapnel shells, a strong effect on morale was noted, which forced the crews of the enemy aircraft to spurn the fulfillment of the assigned mission.

It is important to note that in the number of enemy aircraft brought down by infantry fire means, there were not only obsolete, slow-running types of aircraft, but also a significant number of modern, fast-moving fighter aircraft and bombers (Me-109, Me-110, Ju-88, Makki-200).

Thus, firing by infantry from rifles, light machine guns, antitank rifles, and 76mm guns against dive bombers and low-flying aircraft is a very effective means of combat. These infantry fire tactics often force enemy aircraft to give up completely on attacking infantry or to conduct the attack at an altitude which is out of the zone of effective infantry fire, thus significantly reducing the effectiveness of the attack.

The enemy himself acknowledges the success of the struggle of our infantry against his aircraft. Thus, in one of the captured orders from the German 6th Army the following was written: "Our air force reports that Soviet troops are meeting our ground-level flying aircraft with defensive fire from machine guns, thus inflicting perceptible losses and damage on us." The unanswered assault attacks of Soviet aircraft were noted further on in the order, and in conclusion it was stated that, "all soldiers must open fire with rifles and machine guns against ground-level flying enemy aircraft."

Unfortunately, not all commanders and staffs of units and formations appreciate sufficiently these infantry fire means. One still encounters units which, at the appearance of enemy aviation, limit themselves to camouflage measures or the conduct of disorderly fire with little effect. One also finds units in which training of soldiers in the application of infantry gun fire against enemy aircraft is not undertaken, and is not organized. Nevertheless, the experience of combat actions clearly demonstrates that where the training of soldiers in firing against air targets was given sufficient attention, and where this fire was capably organized, there could be counted a large number of downed enemy aircraft, the activity of enemy aviation was made more difficult, and the troops suffered significantly fewer losses from air attacks.

The experience of the combat use of infantry fire means against air targets showed that the most advantageous distances for firing against enemy aircraft are the following:

- up to 500 meters for rifles and light machine guns;
- up to 800 meters for antitank guns;
- up to 1.5–2 kilometers for 76mm guns under conditions of a flank flight of the target, i.e., at a target distance of 1.5–2 kilometers and an altitude of no more than 700 meters.

Thus, with its fire means the infantry can fight against enemy aircraft exclusively at low altitudes of 400–700 meters. In the zone of effective infantry fire enemy aviation will, most often, attempt the following flights:

1. Ground attack flights (*shturmovoi polet*), carried out at altitudes of 30–100 meters. Short time intervals, both from the moment of the appearance of the airplane to the moment of its entrance into the zone of effective fire, and of its passage through the fire zone (5–9

seconds), with large angles of parallax, are characteristic in the fight against ground attack aircraft. Enemy ground attack aircraft in their flight in the immediate vicinity of the soldiers or to the side at a distance of 400–450 meters can be shot down by small-arms fire. In firing against aircraft it is necessary to remember that if one's troops are to the side at a distance of 2–3 kilometers, then it is dangerous to fire with angles of sight of up to 15 degrees, since the bullet at the point of contact with the ground still has lethal power.

2. Bomber flights (*polet bombardirovshchikov*), which attack while diving. As a rule, enemy aircraft approach the target at middle and high altitudes, maximally using camouflage means (clouds, flight to the target from the direction of the sun). A bomber attack occurs in the following way. Individual airplanes (one after the other) from an altitude of 1,500–2,000 meters go into a dive. The airplane, after moving away from the target in front of an approaching airplane, drops its bombs with respect to its altitude: in a sharp dive (60–85 degrees), 500–600 meters; with a sloped dive (45–60 degrees), 200 meters. Having dropped its bombs, it leaves the target at maximum speed with loss in altitude, often in a contour flight using the terrain profile. The threat of an air attack by dive bombers can be detected, with a good organization of observation service, 40–60 seconds before the moment of the entry of the airplane into the zone of effective infantry fire; this time is sufficient to encounter the dive bombers. The time for the dive bombers to pass through the zone of effective fire will be very short, as it was for the ground attack flight; but the angles of parallax of the air targets at the moment of the dive and while the aircraft is coming out of it (under conditions of diving at those firing or at a point located in their immediate vicinity) will be close to 0 degrees, which makes the conditions most favorable for firing.

3. Flights of individual aircraft, most often reconnaissance, under conditions of dense low clouds up to 200 meters. The flight to the target or objective is carried out in or behind the clouds, with a subsequent exit from them for a short time. This particular type of flight is encountered comparatively rarely and is not typical for fighting against them by infantry means.

Proceeding from the conditions of the flights of enemy aircraft at low altitudes, one can indicate the following general reasons which make it difficult to conduct infantry fire in all cases:

- brief time from the moment of detecting the aircraft until the moment of opening fire, especially with assault attacks;
- brevity of the airplane's remaining in the infantry fire zone;
- large angles of shift of the air targets;
- strong effect on soldier morale rendered by the airplane's executing an attack at low altitude.

For infantry fire means to successfully fight against enemy aircraft, the following are necessary:

1. Careful organization of air observation and timely notification of troops concerning air danger.
2. Capable ranging from weapons which do not have special sights for firing against air targets.
3. Use of the most effective shells and rounds in firing against air targets.
4. Conduct of organized fire by individual soldiers and groups.

Air observation and notification of troops concerning an air raid should be organized so that it not only excludes the possibility of a surprise attack, but also allows time (not less than 30–40 seconds) for the troops to be dispersed and occupy their positions for firing. Consequently, the troops should be informed about the direction of the air danger when enemy airplanes are located 4–5 kilometers away. In accordance with this, the location of the air observation posts should also be no less than this distance.

Air observation should be all-round. It is necessary to give special attention to an examination of the edges of forests, hollows, and other folds in the terrain, since they are the primary directions for hedge-hopping aircraft flights. It is expedient to set up individual air observers on these directions, in addition to the existing system of air observation posts, at a distance which would guarantee the timely notification of troops concerning a threat of air attack (up to 2–2.5 kilometers). This is especially necessary on the march, when troops are most often subject to surprise assault attack, sometimes suffering significant losses. A soldier assigned to air observation must be able to identify enemy airplanes well; he must have goggles (dark glasses) and means for signaling.

The simplest means for signaling air danger are visual means (rockets, flags). When the observer's distance from the troops is beyond the limits of visibility of the signal being given, then it is necessary to set up intermediate posts for relaying the signal being given by the observer.

Ranging is the most complex element in conducting fire against enemy airplanes because of the brevity of their remaining in the fire zone, the large angular shift of the air targets in relation to the firing, and the rapid change in the distances of the firing. Available experience in the fight against enemy aviation by means of small-arms fire, and theoretical calculations give a foundation on which to conclude that in firing from rifles and machine guns, the sight setting for all distances in the zone of effective fire should be "3". In firing with such a sight setting, with ranging in the center of the vital part of the aircraft, the bullet trajectory over the entire expanse of the zone of effective fire (500 meters) does not leave the limits of the area of the vital part of the aircraft (direct shot).

An aim off in the direction of the motion of the aircraft to a value equal to the path traversed by the aircraft during the time of the bullet's flight (lead) is most complex. Lead, depending on the distance of the firing and speed and path of the aircraft, has significant linear and angular values which have a great influence on the probability of a hit; this cannot be substituted by some average value. In each concrete instance, depending on the reasons indicated above, the angular value of the lead will be different, and, consequently, the aim off will also be different.

In the practice of firing against airplanes from rifles and machine guns, the

Table of Aim Off in Firing Against Enemy Aircraft from Rifles and Machine Guns

1. Me-109 fighter:
   100 meters - 2
   200 meters - 4
   300 meters - 6.5
   400 meters - 9
   500 meters - 11.5
   600 meters - 14

2. Khe-113 fighter:
   100 meters - 2
   200 meters - 4.5
   300 meters - 7
   400 meters - 10
   500 meters - 13
   600 meters - 16

3. Me-110 twin-engine fighter:
   100 meters - 1.5
   200 meters - 3
   300 meters - 5
   400 meters - 7
   500 meters - 9
   600 meters - 12

4. Ju-88, Ju-87, Do-215, Khe-111 bombers; KhSh-126 observation aircraft:
   100 meters - 1
   200 meters - 2
   300 meters - 3
   400 meters - 4
   500 meters - 5.5
   600 meters - 7

5. KhSh-125 dive bomber:
   100 meters - 1.2
   200 meters - 2.5
   300 meters - 4
   400 meters - 5.5
   500 meters - 7
   600 meters - 9

6. Do-19 heavy bomber:
   100 meters - 0.5
   200 meters - 1
   300 meters - 1.5
   400 meters - 2
   500 meters - 3
   600 meters - 3.5

so-called fuselage method of aim off has justified itself the most. According to this method, the ranging point is aimed off by means of putting off a specific quantity of fuselage of the aircraft, calculated beforehand, along its line of motion. Calculated values for aim off in fuselages for various aircraft and distances are given in the table on the preceding page.

All commanders and soldiers must always carry this table and memorize the basic data on aim off in firing against enemy airplanes passing in their direction.

An exception to the mentioned type of ranging is firing against an enemy airplane which is diving directly at the gunner. A feature in this case is the absence of an angle of parallax of the airplane, which creates most favorable conditions for firing from the point of view of simplicity in ranging (direct laying in the propeller sleeve of the aircraft) and the great probability of a hit.

When firing with a light machine gun it is expedient for correcting fire to use one round with a tracer bullet across every two–three conventional or special rounds.

When firing with a 76mm gun and with a flank flight of enemy aircraft at an altitude of 700 meters and a distance of 1,500 meters, it is necessary to conduct fire without instruments, aiming off along the line of flight on three fuselages and giving the gun a quadrant elevation of 45–50 degrees; and to fire shrapnel, using a T-6 tube with a mounting of 25.

For firing against air targets from antitank guns, a special antiaircraft sight and tripod were developed; these have begun to appear among the troops.

In the practice of troop combat actions, there are a number of examples of well-thought-out organization of the fight against enemy aviation using infantry fire means. In one army of the Kalinin Front, mobile groups of massed small-arms fire for fighting against enemy aviation were created; these groups were outfitted with snipers and formed into squads and platoons. The mobile groups moved on the most probable directions of enemy aircraft flight and created powerful small-arms fire. In one month of combat work by these mobile groups, 20 enemy aircraft were brought down.

The reinforcement of individual air defense targets by gun and machine gun subunits has also provided good results.

The most widespread variant in organizing the fight against enemy aviation using infantry means is the assignment of squads, platoons, and sometimes companies into units and subunits. These subunits are distributed on the probable directions of enemy aircraft flight and prepare their fire positions quickly. During an air attack they conduct fire against enemy airplanes, and the rest of the time they carry out usual combat missions. It is expedient to equip these subunits with small-arms fire marksmen, specially preparing them to fire against airplanes using hand guns.

There are many variants in organizing the fight against enemy aviation, but the main thing is that the commanders, in making their decision, assign concrete missions to the subunits for using infantry fire means to fight against enemy aircraft.

Commanders at all levels must show particular concern for the training of all personnel in conducting fire against air targets. In the course of the training, together with working out the elements of ranging and determining distances, it is also necessary to give serious attention to the choice of soldiers, especially machine gunners, and fire positions. It is necessary to remember that the fire position is chosen independently by the soldiers in a very limited period of time, most often on unfamiliar terrain. On such terrain the soldier must use everything that can help facilitate his conduct of fire against aircraft – local objects, unevenness, etc. – and it is necessary to systematically train soldiers for this.

However, one training session for firing does not guarantee a successful fight against enemy aviation; it is necessary to capably control fire in squads, platoons, and sometimes companies at the appearance of enemy aircraft, and fire discipline is also necessary. Before producing a shot it is necessary to determine the type of airplane, distance to the target, and aim off on the fuselage; and all this must be done in an extremely short period of time. This complexity in firing often forces soldiers to conduct disorderly fire without ranging or with an incorrect aim off. The commander must introduce a sense of organization into the conduct of fire by giving brief commands determining the moment of the commencement and conclusion of the conduct of fire, and the value of the aim off on the aircraft fuselage; the commander must concentrate all his attention on determining the initial data for firing. In addition, it is necessary to take into consideration the fact that assault attacks of enemy aircraft, as well as diving attacks, have a strong effect on the soldiers' morale, prompting them to hide behind cover. In this case the commands given by the commander have the significance of encouragement and introduce a sense of organization into the conduct of fire.

In the fight against enemy aviation, infantry fire means are widely used by the troops. It is necessary to develop and improve in every way possible these means, which have grown on the battlefields of the Great

Patriotic War into an awesome force for the destruction of fascist aircraft. For this it is necessary to improve equipment for firing against enemy aircraft on the basis of a detailed study of the experience of fighting against enemy aviation by commanders at all levels, and to organize an exchange of this valuable experience among units and subunits of the Red Army.

The Experience of Conducting an Operational War Game on the Front

At the beginning of the current year, an operational, unilateral war game was conducted by one of the field armies on the front of the Great Patriotic War; it was conducted using maps and the terrain, with communications means, on the theme "The defensive battle at the boundary of two armies with a counterattack from the depth". In addition to the army apparatus which organized the game, commanders and chiefs of staff of one rifle corps, four rifle divisions, one motorized rifle division, five rifle brigades, two tank brigades, and one air division took part in this war game.

The positive significance of the war game from the point of view of combining combat work with training should be noted. The Military Council of the army, which organized the war game, correctly and capably used a lull on the front for the purpose of preparing commanders and chiefs of staff of formations for forthcoming combat actions, and developing in them a uniform understanding of and coordination in resolving combat missions.

Although it is not possible to analyze in detail the dynamics of the war game, we will focus our attention on problems of organizing and preparing materials for the war game, which are of great practical interest.

I. THEMES AND TRAINING GOALS

The theme of the war game fully corresponded to the conditions of the situation created on the given sector of the front. It included one of the most important elements of the mission being executed by the army – fighting at a boundary with a neighboring unit in combination with a counterattack of operational reserves.

The basis of the operational plan was the sharpest features of the possible variants of activity of the actual enemy, arising from reconnaissance data on the regroupings and concentrations of the latter, as well as from a consideration of terrain conditions.

The training goals were established as the following:

1. To impart to commanders and staffs stability in defensive battles against superior enemy forces.

2. To train commanders and staffs to organize control capably and to correctly use second combat echelons and antitank reserves in the fight against airborne assaults;
3. To work out the commitment of operational reserves for a counterstrike at the moment of going over from the defense to the offense.
4. To train them in mastering the organization and tactics of the enemy.

The situation in relation to the position of the enemy and one's own troops, the terrain, and the arrangement of headquarters and command posts was taken as actual, with the exception of some deviations in relation to enemy strength and deployment, necessary to create the needed superiority. The compilation of initial data for conducting the war game did not cause special difficulties and did not require much time under conditions of the combat situation.

Thus, the Military Council of the army approached the organization of the war game in a sufficiently well thought-out manner. All the possibilities for bringing the participants of the war game close to the actual situation were used. There was nothing devised, nothing which forced them to lose touch with the situation that had actually unfolded; moreover, in the course of the game several units were enlisted to carry out individual combat missions.

The initial data for the participants in the operational war game, worked out by the army staffs, included the overall situation with an indication of what must be completed by the beginning of the game; a map of the position of the sides; and lists of the participants.

In addition, a plan for conducting the game, with the plan of enemy action depicted on the map, was worked out for the leadership and mediators.

II. SITUATION BY THE CLOSE OF 4 SEPTEMBER 1941
(SKETCH 1)

1. The position of our troops and enemy troops by the close of 4 September 1941 – relative to the position occupied on the front.

    The 57th Army, consisting of the 12th, 5th, and 34th Rifle Divisions, has the mission of defending the line on the eastern bank and holding the bridgehead occupied on the western bank of the Vyrva River.

    On the right the 8th Rifle Division of the 2d Army is defending; the boundary with it is (excluding) Stepanovo, (excluding) Volino.

    On the left the 152d Rifle Division of the 6th Army is defending; the boundary with it is the former one.

2. On 3 and 4 September, strong enemy fire activity was noted on the sectors of the 5th and 34th Rifle Divisions; continuous artillery and mortar raids against the regions: Khvatovo, Ilino; Khramovo; Vlasovo, Luchki and Borki, Ekhovka.

On these days enemy reconnaissance was active in the directions of Ilino and Ekhovka.

On the sector of the 12th Rifle Division it was comparatively calm on 3 and 4 September. The enemy conducted occasional artillery and mortar fire and strengthened its reconnaissance activity.

According to unverified data, the enemy mined individual sectors in the area of Borki, Grishino, and made passages in the barbed wire obstacles.

3. From neighboring units the following was known:
   - it was relatively calm on the right flank of the 2d Army; occasional artillery and mortar fire was being conducted. On the sector of the 135th Rifle Division the enemy, on 3 and 4 September, conducted fierce artillery and mortar fire against the regions of Stukovo and Orekhovo. Enemy reconnaissance penetrated to the western outskirts of Sychevo;
   - there was occasional artillery and mortar fire on the front of the 8th Rifle Division;
   - according to information from prisoners, the enemy mined individual sectors and removed the barbed wire in the area west of Danilkovo, Borki;
   - the enemy conducted powerful artillery and mortar raids against the right flank of the division on the front of the 152d Rifle Division of the 6th Army. His reconnaissance attempted to penetrate beyond the forward edge of the defense, but it was completely destroyed. According to documents of the dead men, the actions on this front were corroborated by the 138th Infantry Division of the enemy.

4. According to air reconnaissance data it is certain that since the second half of August intensified movement of trains has been observed from the west to Krasnoe, as has the unloading of troops in the area of Krasnoe. The arrival of troop trains continues.

At the same time, vehicular transport and concentration of troops were observed in the area of Somovo and the grove west of Vorob'evo. In the area Sukhovo, Ilovo, there has been an accumulation of tanks and motor vehicles. All these regions are strongly covered by antiaircraft artillery.

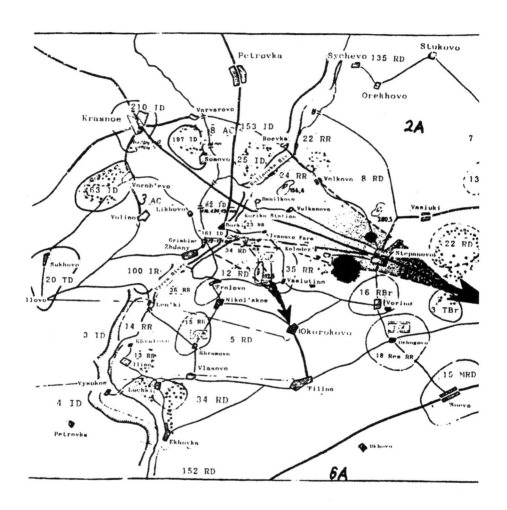

Sketch 1: Position of the sides by the close of 4 September 1941 and enemy plan

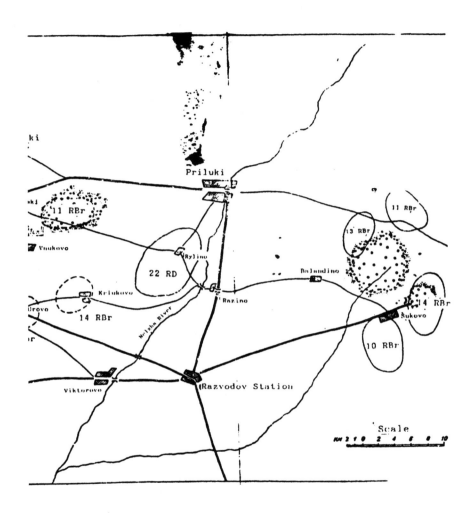

On 2 and 3 September air reconnaissance detected the construction of crossings across the Vyrva River in the areas: east of the outskirts of Varvarovo, 200 meters north of Somovo, between the railroad and the mouth of the Kalinovka River, southeast of the edge of the forest, north of Likhovo and north of the outskirts of Grishino.

The areas of the crossings are covered by antiaircraft artillery. Our artillery conducted fire against these crossings and partially destroyed them. According to the reports of the flight crews who were reconnoitering this area, the crossings were re-established.

5. From the interrogation of captured prisoners and from captured documents in the period 25–31 August on the sectors of the 8th and 12th Rifle Divisions, the following was established:

    –   The presence of units of the enemy 153d Infantry Division (prisoner captured one kilometer north of Roevka) and the 82d Infantry Division (prisoner taken in the grove north of Borki) before the front of the 8th Rifle Division;

    –   the 12th Rifle Division south of Zhdany captured a prisoner of the 121st Infantry Regiment of the 161st Infantry Division;

    –   at the end of August, units of the 153d, 82d, and 161st Infantry Divisions were replenished with personnel and arms, as much as 75 per cent and 50 per cent of the organic make-up respectively.

6. The command point of the 57th Army is Ozhogovo.

Order: 1. The beginning of the war game is 0400, 5 September 1941.

       2. By the beginning of the war game the participants are obliged to do the following:

          – study the situation and analyze it;

          – know the organization of the units and formations of the German army;

          – (commanders of the 8th and 12th Rifle Divisions) write a combat report to the Military Council of the army.

III. PLAN OF CONDUCT OF THE OPERATIONAL WAR GAME
5–6 SEPTEMBER 1941*

Date and Time

Astronomical – 5 September, 0400–1200
Operational – 5 September, 0400–2400

*Translator's note: tabular form in original text.

Stage of the Game

Defensive battle.

Enemy Actions

At 0500 the enemy began artillery preparation. Strong artillery and mortar fire was concentrated against the following areas: Volkovo and the grove to the north; hill 156.4, Danilkovo; Vulkanovo, Korino station; Ivanovo farm and the grove to the south; hill 112.5, Frolovo.

From 0500 these areas were subjected to strong air attacks.

At 0700, the 153d, 25th, 82d, and 161st Infantry Divisions went over to the offensive on the front Roevka, Grishino, inflicting the main strike of the 153d, 25th, and 82d Infantry Divisions and 20th Tank Division from the front Roevka, Danilkovo in the general direction of Stepanovo, and an auxiliary strike of the 161st Infantry Division on the front Borki, Grishino, on the axis Vasiutino, Okorokovo.

For the development of success, the 197th and 63rd Infantry Divisions are in the second echelon on the front Varvarovo, Vorob'evo.

All these forces are part of the 8th Army Corps (153d, 25th, and 197th Infantry Divisions) and the 3d Army Corps (161st, 82d, and 63d Infantry Divisions); the 20th Tank Division is subordinate to the 8th Army Corps.

Hypothetical Situations

1. At 0500 on 5 September the enemy dropped a parachute assault at a strength of up to two battalions (around 1,000 men) with mortars and machine guns into the area of the grove northwest of Urovo.
2. From 0530 groups of 15–20 airplanes each bomb Stepanovo, Okorokovo, Vorino, Ozhogovo, Soevo, Razvodovo station; the bridge across the Nelzha River near Viktorovo has been destroyed.
3. All lines of communication have been destroyed.
4. At 1200 the enemy at a strength of up to two regiments with one tank company has crossed to the eastern shore of the Kalinovka River, 1.5 kilometers south of Roevka, and has penetrated 500–600 meters into our defense. Over the entire remaining front the 8th Rifle Division is engaged in fierce battles on the forward edge.
5. At 1200 on the front, the 12th Rifle Division is engaged in a strong battle on the forward edge. Up to two enemy regiments with a tank company have captured the western and northwestern edge of the grove (southwest of Ivanovo farm).
6. At 1400, tanks are crossing the Kalinovka River in the area 1.5 kilometers south of Roevka (data of the forward units of the 8th Rifle Division).

7. At 1500, air reconnaissance established the movement of two tank columns: one is up to 50 tanks moving eastward, with the head southwest of the outskirts of Roevka; the other, up to 30 tanks, has crossed the Vyrva River north of Grishino.

Work of the Game Participants (corresponding to the hypothetical situations)

1. Evaluation of the situation by the commanders of the 8th and 12th Rifle Divisions, orders given to the units; processing reports at army headquarters (note: forces and means from the 22d Rifle Division to check combat readiness and time calculations).
2. Dispatching a detachment to fight against the air assault.
3. Transmission of orders and reports only by radio (radio signals by telephone).
4. Decision of the commander of the 8th Rifle Division, transmission of order to the units and the report to *ShTARM* (*shtab armii*/army headquarters).
5. Decision of the commander of the 12th Rifle Division, transmission of order to the units and the report to army headquarters.
6. Decision-making by the commanders of the 1st Rifle Corps and 15th Motorized Rifle Division on the march. Formulation of the order. March calculation. Report to army headquarters (note: the order of the army commander is transmitted at 0500 on 5 September orally by communications officers; see situation map for areas of concentration).

Date and Time
Astronomical – 1200–1800, 5 September
Operational – 0000–2400, 6 September

Stage of the Game
Defensive battle.

Enemy Actions

1. Having penetrated the front in the area of Roevka and the grove south of Ivanovo farm, the enemy introduced a tank division into the penetration and by the close of 6 September occupied the following:
   - 153d Infantry Division with 20 tanks – Vasiuki, hill 280.5; attempting to capture Stepanovo;
   - 82d Infantry Division with 10 tanks – Trelino; developing the offensive in the direction of the railroad;
   - 161st and 63d Infantry Division with a tank group consisting of

30–40 tanks – the grove south of Trelino, Vasiutino.

Over the course of 5–6 September, the enemy suffered the following losses:
- 153d Infantry Division – as much as 40%;
- 82d Infantry Division – as much as 50%;
- 161st Infantry Division – completely routed;
- 63d Infantry Division – as much as 30%;
- 20th Tank Division – as much as 60%.

2. The 138th Infantry Division was not successful and continues to conduct battle on the forward edge.

3. The reserve of the 197th Infantry Division and the 201st Infantry Division, newly arrived in the area of Krasnoe, engaged in battle from the morning of 7 September, the 197th in the direction of Stepanovo, the 201st in the direction of Vasiutino, Vorino.

4. Over the course of the entire day, enemy aviation operated on the battlefield and against massing of troops.

Hypothetical Situations

1. At 2300, 5 September, the enemy occupied Volkovo, Vulkanovo, and the grove south of Ivanovo farm.

2. At 0600 air reconnaissance reported the following:
- troops continue to be unloaded at Krasnoe Station;
- movement of an infantry column with artillery – the head is at Roevka, the tail at Varvarovo;
- movement of an infantry column with artillery – the head is 500 meters west of Borki, the tail at Vorob'evo.

3. At the front of the 5th Rifle Division, the enemy attempted to go over to the offensive, but was beaten back. Prisoners were taken by the 3d Infantry Division.

4. On the front of the 152d Rifle Division, the enemy offensive was also unsuccessful.

5. By 1200 on 6 September, the position of the units was as follows:
- 8th Rifle Division: 22d Rifle Regiment is holding the initial position. All enemy attacks have been repelled. The 23d Rifle Regiment, by means of two battalions, is conducting battle in encirclement (area dependent on the decision of the players); 24th Rifle Regiment, having suffered great losses, is conducting battle northwest of Stepanovo;
- 12th Rifle Division: 36th Rifle Regiment is holding the initial position. The 34th and 35th Rifle Regiments, suffering great losses

and fighting an intense battle, are forced to withdraw.

6. Give the position by the close of 6 September (see point 1 on the graph – "Enemy actions").

Work of the Game Participants

1. Play through the organization of the march of the 1st Rifle Corps, 15th Mechanized Division, and 3d Tank Brigade.
2. Decision of the commanders of the 8th and 12th Rifle Divisions on the course of the situation.
3. Transfer of the command position.
4. Play through the battle in the antitank areas on the sectors of the 8th and 12th Rifle Divisions.
5. Artillery (division and army) maneuver.
6. Organization and conduct of tank reconnaissance.
7. Evaluation by all players of the situation by 2400, 6 September.
8. Order of the commander of the army on the engagement of the 1st Rifle Corps, 15th Motorized Rifle Division, and 3d Tank Brigade into battle (0500, 6 September, operational time).

Date and Time

Astronomical – 1800–2400, 5 September
Operational – 0000–0600, 7 September

Stage of the Game

Engagement of operational reserves into battle.

Enemy Actions

1. Further enemy actions on the morning of 7 September were not successful.
2. At 1000, the 197th Infantry Division is engaged on the direction hill 280.5, Stepanovo; the 201st Rifle Division is engaged on the direction Vasiutino, Vorino.

    By 0600 on 7 September, the main forces of these divisions are located as follows:
    –   197th Rifle Division – 2 kilometers east of Volkovo;
    –   201st Rifle Division – Kolodez'.

Hypothetical Situation

1. Data of air reconnaissance on the approach of the 197th and 201st Rifle Divisions.
2. 3d Tank Brigade engaged in battle.

44

THE EXPERIENCE OF CONDUCTING AN OPERATIONAL WAR GAME

Work of the Game Participants
1. Evaluation of the situation by 0600, 7 September.
2. Order of the commander of the 1st Rifle Corps, 22d Rifle Division, 10th, 11th, 13th, and 14th Rifle Brigades, 3d and 7th Tank Brigades, and 15th Motorized Rifle Division.
3. Organization of interaction between combat arms.
4. Organization of control.
5. Playing through the battle of the 23d Rifle Regiment in encirclement.

Date and Time
Astronomical – 0400–1500, 6 September
Operational – 0600–1200, 7 September

Stage of the Game
Engagement of operational reserves into battle.

Enemy Actions
The 197th and 201st Infantry Divisions enter into battle.

Hypothetical Situations
1. Aviation inflicts strikes against the operational reserves with their advance from the line of departure.
2. Engagement of 1st Rifle Corps and 15th Motorized Rifle Division into battle.

Work of the Game Participants
1. Organization of counterstrike of the 1st Rifle Corps, 15th Motorized Rifle Division, and 3d Tank Brigade.
2. Play through the battle.
3. Control.

Date and Time
Astronomical – 0400–1500, 6 September
Operational – 1200–2000, 7 September

Stage of the Game
Engagement of operational reserves into battle.

Enemy Actions
Withdrawal of formation which had penetrated.

Hypothetical Situations

By the close of 7 September the position on the front of the 8th and 12th Rifle Divisions has been completely re-established.

Work of the Game Participants

Organization of pursuit of the withdrawing enemy.

Date and Time

Astronomical – 0400–1500, 6 September
Operational – 2000 (7 September)–0600 (8 September)

Stage of the Game

Going over to the offensive.

Enemy Actions

Attempt to hold on the forward defensive line.

Hypothetical Situations

1. Position of the units by the morning of 8 September will be given by the leadership depending on the decision of the players.
2. Players given the order of the commander of the army for the offensive.

Work of the Game Participants

1. Formulation of the orders of the commanders of formations for the offensive.
2. Organization of interaction.
3. Organization of control.

Date and Time

Astronomical – 1500, 6 September

Stage of the Game

Sign off.

Date and Time

Astronomical – 2000, 6 September

Stage of the Game

Analysis of the war game.

THE EXPERIENCE OF CONDUCTING AN OPERATIONAL WAR GAME

Work of the Game Participants

Assembly of the game participants at the command post of army headquarters.

IV. ORGANIZATION OF THE WAR GAME

After processing the training documents, preparation of the leadership and umpires for the war game, including travel to the terrain, took place over five days. In the course of the preparation, all questions connected with the conduct of the war game were treated in detail on maps and on the terrain, which provided high quality training and interest on the part of the participants.

Five days may seem too long for preparation; however, it is necessary to keep in mind that the preparation proceeded without taking away many commanders from troop control, and was connected with the leaders visiting a significant number of command posts and large sectors of the terrain.

In addition to the aforementioned training documents, army headquarters developed procedure tables and lists of the war game participants and umpires with the headquarters of the formations.

Taking into consideration the conditions of the combat situation, special attention was given to the selection of war game participants. In the organization of the war game, the leadership took into account that the "lull" in the combat situation was relative, that during this period, although there were no serious combat actions, the combat actions of the troops continued, as it was necessary to be uninterruptedly in charge of such activity. Therefore, removing a large number of responsible commanders could be harmfully reflected in troop actions and create an uneasy situation for the players.

For the purpose of combining the interests of the combat situation and those of the war game, army headquarters developed personal lists of participants with respect to all the formations. In compiling the lists, the features of the combat situation before the front of each formation were, above all, taken into consideration, and only after this were the necessary personnel allotted for participation in the war game.

With such a selection of participants, it was, naturally, impossible for all the formations to work through the noted training goals and episodes. Therefore, before the commencement of the war game, the leadership completely and correctly determined the degree of depth of working through the training goals in each formation. Thus, for example, in the 8th Rifle Division the division engineer could not be enlisted to participate in the war game because of the conditions of the combat situation; in this division the problems of engineer support of troops in the defense had to be worked out in general terms; however, this problem had to be worked out in detail in the 12th Rifle Division, where the division engineer was able to participate in the war game. These foreseen gaps in working through the training goals, characteristic for each formation individually, were "filled in" during the analysis.

In playing through the various episodes with the umpires, they received detailed instruction on problems of the depth of working through the training goals with respect to the various formations, based on the composition of the game participants.

Thus, an all-round, well thought-out selection of participants and careful preparation of the war game provided the command with a sufficiently full treatment of the assigned training goals in a calm situation for the players (there were no instances of removing the game participants).

It should be noted that the great interest attached by the command to the war game was completely supported by all the participants. In the course of the war game the commanders capably made use of all new devices for fighting which had developed on the battlefields of the Great Patriotic War. Among these devices were completely new ones which had yet to be widely disseminated but were already verified in a combat situation.

Everything new from the combat practice of the troops and brought out by the war game was used by the command at the analysis as an exchange of combat experience. It should be acknowledged that the exchange of combat experience as a result of the operational war game was a very valuable supplementary training–educational exercise for the commanders who participated.

Stalin's First of May order established as one of the primary missions: "combined arms commanders must study completely the matter of interaction of the combat arms, become experts in the matter of troop leadership, and show the whole world that the Red Army is capable of fulfilling its great mission of liberation!"

In fulfilling the mission assigned by the People's Commissariat for Defense, commanders at all levels who are located at the front must use everything possible to train their subordinates in a combat situation as well.

The analyzed example of organization and preparation of a war game gives a foundation for making a conclusion about the possibility of such training under corresponding conditions of a combat situation.

The German Field Defense

The review was compiled from materials of the active Red Army's offensive battles of 1941–42. The main content of the review is an acquaintanceship with the fundamental principles of the structure of the German defense from the point of view of use of terrain and its reinforcement by means of field fortification; at the same time the fundamentals of German tactics on the defense are set forth.

The fundamental principles of the structure of the German defense are predominantly analyzed in their use by the Germans on the "main battlefield" (the primary defensive zone of the German tactical zone of defense). Problems of the German Army's operational defense are treated only in connection with determining the area which occupies the "main battlefield" in the general scheme of the German defense.

I. GENERAL POSITIONS

The Germans bind the system of defense to populated areas, commanding heights, and tactically advantageous terrain profiles; they structure their defense as dependent on their presence and arrangement. The connection of the German defense to populated areas was expressed especially clearly in the winter.

The German defense is mainly based on a system of separate pockets of resistance (strong points, centers of resistance) equipped for an all-round defense and located within mutual fire support.

The gaps between the centers of resistance and strong points are covered by fire, often covered by obstacles, and are necessarily patrolled.

In the organization of the defense, great significance is attached to the terrain. Fire means are carefully deployed on the terrain, taking into consideration camouflage and the conduct of indirect and flank fire.

The tactical zone of the German defense usually consists of 2 defensive zones with an overall depth of 10–15 kilometers. The primary defense forces are concentrated on the first (primary) defensive zone, which the Germans call the "main battlefield". The depth of this zone is an average of 4–5

49

kilometers, including the artillery fire positions. The second defensive zone of the tactical zone of defense serves to create depth and, as a rule, is not occupied by troops. Sometimes it is occupied by reserves which, in anticipation of the transfer of the defense to this zone, bring it to combat readiness in advance.

According to German opinions, the defense is transferred from the primary zone to the second zone when the resistance of the "main battlefield" troops in the first defensive zone is broken, and the engagement of reserves is connected with incommensurately great sacrifices (p. 451 of the Regulations, "Troop Leadership").

The terrain between the defense zones is poorly saturated with fire means. Here separate strong points and points of reinforcement are usually located to protect the rear of the divisions and headquarters from the actions of our partisans and Red Army units which have made their way into the rear. In addition, the first and second defense zones are joined by alternative positions (in German terminology, flank positions).

The practical experience of battles shows that if the Germans decide to use a rigid defense on a given line, then they engage all their forces, right up to the army reserves, in the battle for the main battlefield, removing units from other sectors of the front to this direction.

It should be noted that German regulations require that the main battlefield be held "until the very end".

In the depth, the German operational defense had defensive lines, usually prepared beforehand by the local population. The completion of the outfitting of these lines was successfully done by the troops themselves as soon as the necessity to withdraw them to new lines was determined.

In addition, air defense means and separate pockets of defense covering important military targets (bridges, railroad junctions, road junctions, etc.) were deployed in the operational depth of the German defense.

The frequent attacks of our partisans against various important military targets in the enemy rear forced the Germans to have strong direct protection and often to construct various field fortification structures to protect these targets.

The principal diagram of the German operational defense is shown in Sketch 2.

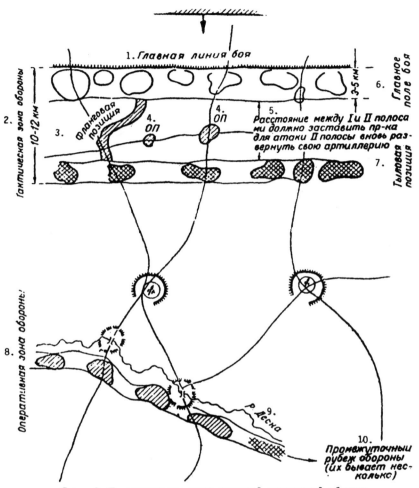

Схема 2. Принципиальная схема немецкой оперативной обороны

Sketch 2. Principal sketch of the German Operational Defense

1. Main line of battle
2. Tactical zone of defense
3. Flank position
4. Strong point
5. Distance between zones I and II should force the enemy to deploy his artillery again to attack zone II

6. Main battlefield
7. Rear position
8. Operational zone of defense
9. Desna River
10. Intermediate line of defense (there are several)

51

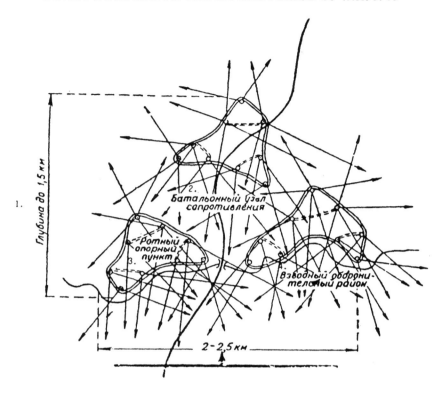

Sketch 3.   Center of Resistance

1. Depth of up to 1.5 kilometers
2. Battalion center of resistance
3. Company strong point
4. Platoon defensive region

II. SYSTEM OF GERMAN DEFENSE ON THE PRIMARY DEFENSE ZONE ("MAIN BATTLEFIELD")

The primary defense zone of the German defense is usually arranged along natural lines and necessarily includes populated areas. Before the forward edge of the primary defense zone, the terrain is always well examined, making it possible to organize good shelling.

The primary defense zone consists of company strong points and battalion centers of resistance. The gaps between the strong points are covered by a system of flanking fire and crossfire, by automatic weapons, and, in a number of cases, by engineer obstacles. In addition, the gaps are covered by artillery and mortar fire from the depth.

In this respect, the following, taken from an order of the 330th German Infantry Division, dated 29 December 1941, is characteristic:

> In the defense there should be no uninterrupted line. Strong points should be built on commanding heights of the terrain with an all-round defense. Garrisons of the strong points should be reinforced with antitank defense means. It is necessary to take into consideration the breaches formed in the defense zone between the strong points. It is desirable that good shelling and observation can be organized from the strong points. But this cannot always be managed; therefore, observation posts should be set up in the gaps between strong points. Breaches in the defense zone between defensive points are not weak areas of the defense – on the contrary, they are left for the enemy so as to destroy him here. The enemy, filtering into these breaches, can be quickly counterattacked and driven back (according to a plan developed beforehand); for this it is necessary to use all available forces, to provide support of the counterattack with heavy weapons and individual artillery guns.

The primary element of the "main battlefield" is the center of resistance. It is independent in the tactical respect and is prepared for a prolonged all-round defense. The center consists of several company strong points connected to each other by a system of flanking fire and crossfire (Sketch 3).

In its turn the company strong point has 2–3 platoon defense regions and includes, in addition to automatic infantry weapons, antitank guns and mortars.

According to opinions of the German Army (order of the 4th Army dated 23 January 1942), the primary defense weapons are machine guns, mortars, and antitank guns. Artillery fire also finds wide application.

The Germans considered the following to be favorable distances for the introduction of fire means into battle in the defense:

- rifle fire and light machine gun fire from 400 meters and closer;
- medium machine guns from 1,000 meters and closer;
- mortar fire from 1 to 3 kilometers.

Fire points, as a rule, are located in structures capable of defense, or

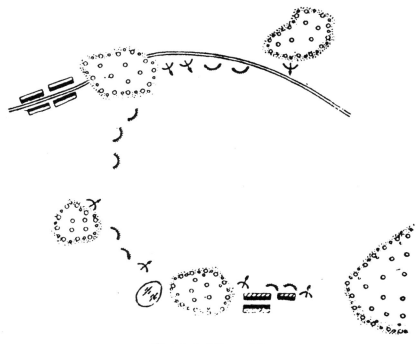

Sketch 4. "Fire sack"

earth-and-timber fire points are built for this purpose. Machine guns set up in trenches on areas covered by overhead protection are also often encountered. The system of fire of a strong point, as well as being a center of resistance, is supplemented by engineer obstacles and, in the first order, mines. All obstacles are necessarily held under intense shelling of the strong point or neighboring strong points.

The roads and approaches to the strong point are carefully mined. A wire net of up to 4 stakes, concertina wire, etc. is placed before the forward edge. In the gaps between the strong points less wire net is unwound (1–2 stakes).

On directions of likely tank approach, in addition to antitank guns, antitank mine fields are set up in the system of strong points; antitank ditches and other passive antitank obstacles are more rarely encountered.

The antitank defense of the German main battlefield relies on fire of the following types:

– supporting artillery, which attempts to bar the path of advancing tanks,

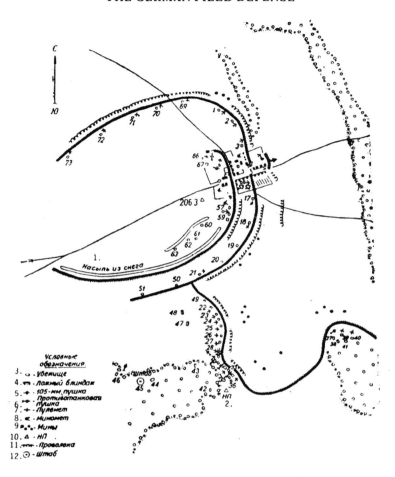

Sketch 5. Sketch of the enemy defense at populated area Mount Ludina

1. Snow embankment
2. Observation point
3. Shelter
4. False dug-out
5. 105-mm cannon
6. Antitank cannon

7. Machine gun
8. Mortar
9. Mines
10. Observation point
11. Wire
12. Staff

beginning from a distance of 3–4 kilometers; fire is primarily conducted using armor-piercing shells;

- antitank guns both of strong points and those guns which are advancing forward and forming an "antitank island;"
- antitank guns, large-caliber machine guns, and machine guns and rifles firing armor-piercing bullets at vision slits.

Advancing tanks which have penetrated into the depth of the defense (according to German instructions, beyond the main battlefield, i.e., beyond the forward edge) are counterattacked by tanks from ambushes and by so-called armor-strike squads (teams of tank fighters).

According to German opinions (instructions for the 502d Infantry Regiment, dated 19 January 1942), in each infantry company there should be 1 armor-strike squad consisting of a sergeant-major (*starshina*), 4 privates, and a sniper. The squad is armed with five 3kg explosive charges, four tank mines, six smoke grenades and Molotov cocktails. The squads operate in the company zone, interacting with an antitank gun, and are usually located in front of its fire position.

In conducting a defensive battle, the defenders attempt by means of concentrated fire and counterattacks to prevent a penetration of the attacker into their forward edge.

In organizing the defense, the Germans usually create "fire sacks" (Sketch 4), the purpose of which is to create the appearance of a weak defense on the given sector, lure the attacking units into it, and, having cut off their path of retreat, destroy them.

"Fire sacks" are usually created between strong points on level, open terrain bordered by forests, hills, and individual structures.

The system of enemy fire is structured on the principle of mutual fire support, flank and crossfire of automatic weapons, massed mortar fire, antitank defense gun fire, and artillery fire from the depth.

On average, the fire density is defined as up to 5 infantry and antitank guns and 1–2 division artillery guns per kilometer of front.

The following principles of the enemy's outfitting of defensive positions can be established from several captured German unit headquarters documents:

1. Position mission – minimal loss of forces and means to achieve the greatest results.
2. The strong point and each structure should have an all-round defense. There should be no patterning in arranging them; great attention should be given to the choice of location for the arrangement of structures.

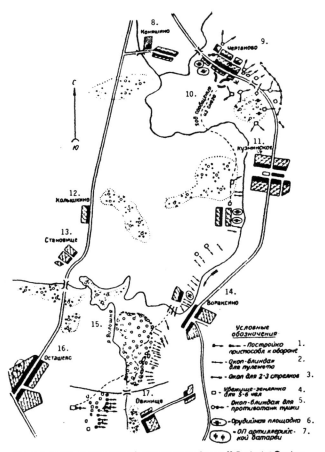

Схема 6. Схема огневых позиций противника на фронте Чертаново — Овинище

Sketch 6. Sketch of enemy fire positions on the Chertanovo–Ovinishche Front

1. Structure adapted for defense
2. Trench-dugout for machine gun
3. Trench for 2–3 gunners
4. Shelter for 5–6 men
5. Trench-dugout for antitank cannon
6. Gun platform
7. Artillery battery strong point
8. Koniashino
9. Chertnovo

10. Communications trench (out of snow)
11. Kuzminskoe
12. Kolyshkino
13. Stanovishche
14. Voraksino
15. Voloshnia River
16. Ostashevo
17. Ovinishche

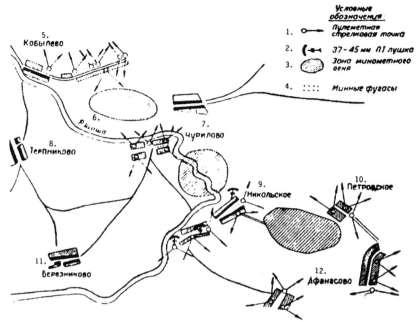

Схема 7. Схема опорного пункта Кобылево — Чурилово — Афанасово

Sketch 7. Sketch of the Kobylevo–Afanasovo strong point

1. Machine gun firing position
2. 37–45-mm antitank cannon
3. Mortar fire zone
4. High explosives (mines)
5. Kobylevo
6. Shosha River

7. Churilovo
8. Terpnikovo
9. Nikol'skoe
10. Petrovskoe
11. Bereznikovo
12. Afanasovo

3. The leading idea in structuring strong posts should be mutual heavy weapons fire support.
4. Strengthening the fire system of the strong points is foreseen by setting up anti-personnel and antitank mines.
5. The designs of the structures should, as a minimum, protect the troops located in them from debris, shells, and mines, and from the possibility of being overrun by tanks. Shelters and command posts must be structured

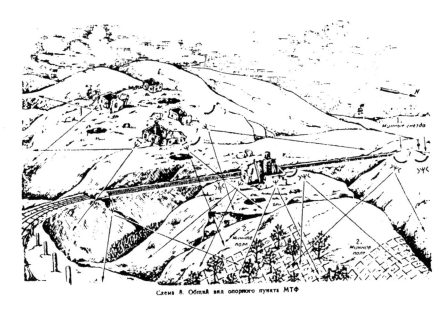

Сдема 8. Общий вид опорного пункта МТФ

Sketch 8. Overall view of a dairy farm strong point

1. Mine nests
2. Mine field

with an all-round defense. Observation points should be located on terrain covered by the structures' general system of fire. Individual structures should be joined in fire groups of up to a reinforced battalion (centers of resistance).

6. Strong points should be joined into centers of resistance. The distance between strong points depends on the terrain conditions and the situation.

7. At first it is foreseen to build simple structures with subsequent reinforcement dependent on time and means.

8. Structures available on the terrain and local materials should be widely used to equip the defense positions. Special emphasis should be placed on the use of cellars in habitable structures and in barns as shelters.

9. It is necessary to select mortar fire positions covertly (behind structures on the opposite slopes), entrench them, and change them often.

10. Special attention should be given to establishment and selection of areas for artillery positions and shelters for teams and ammunition.

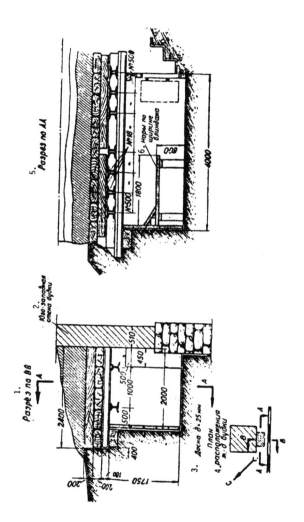

Sketch 9. Dugout built by Germans in a signal box (region of the dairy farm)

1. Section along BB
2. Southwest wall of box
3. Board (d = 25 millimeters)
4. Plan of arrangement of signal box
5. Section along AA
6. Plank bed along width of the dugout

11. Dug-outs should be built with consideration of rapid occupation of fire positions upon an alarm.

III. EXAMPLES OF GERMAN FIELD DEFENSE

1. "Mount Ludina" Center of Resistance (Western Front)

Mount Ludina, the populated area, and hill 206.3 dominate the surrounding terrain on a radius of as much as 10 kilometers. The terrain from here has been closely looked over and well covered by machine gun/rifle fire.

The enemy transformed this area into a powerful center of resistance for the purpose of closing off the passage of our troops west. The entire area was broken from the northeast, east, and southeast into three sectors; the eastern and southeastern were the strongest (Sketch 5).

Having made use of the advantageous position of Mount Ludina, the Germans erected a net of the simplest type reinforcement, and, in conjunction with the natural obstacles, made this mountain difficult for the access of infantry and tanks.

In all, 80 machine gun, 12 mortar and 10 antitank positions were outfitted. In addition, 73 dug-outs were built by the local population; these were joined by communications trenches and had access to the rear. In the immediate vicinity of the dug-outs were trenches for conducting fire.

The dug-outs were easily demolished by 152mm shells.

Fire points were adapted in domiciles and barns, and were also built in the forest and the field.

During the breakthrough, 20 positions, 18 houses, and 5 antitank guns were destroyed.

Mount Ludina was taken from the north, where the enemy least expected the attack. Here was an open field, and the enemy fortified this sector with fewer troops. False attacks from the east and south were simulated on the flanks, distracting the enemy, while, at the same time, the attack from the north was being covertly prepared.

The attack was a complete success, thanks to the correctly chosen direction for the main strike and the careful and covert preparation of all actions.

2. Fire Positions on the Chertanovo–Ovinishche Front (Western Front)

The arrangement of fire means on the Chertanovo–Kuz'minskoe sector was structured according to the principle of group tactics with a shallow depth. In all, 12 machine gun fire positions and 12 gun positions (of which 7 were for antitank guns) were built. The forward edge of the defense, as can be seen

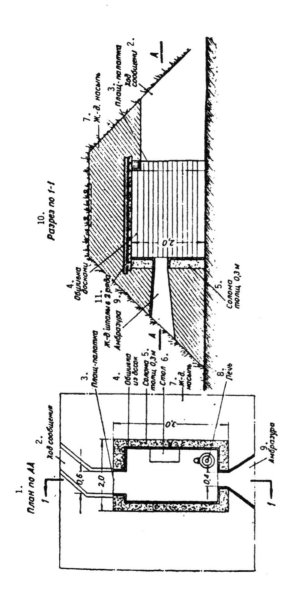

Sketch 10. Sketch of a German earth-and-timber fire point built on a railroad embankment

1. Plan along AA
2. Communications trench
3. Ground sheet
4. Board sheeting

5. Straw, 0.3 meters in thickness
6. Desk
7. Railroad embankment
8. Stove

9. Embrasure
10. Section along 1-1
11. Railroad ties in two rows

from Sketch 6, ran along the road. In the depth, communication trenches were built out of the snow along the entire front.

All structures were of the light type. The adaptation of buildings for conducting fire was widely used. Shelters were usually dug-outs for 5–6 men.

On the Kuz'minskoe–Ovinishche sector, the forward edge ran along the steep western bank of the Voloshnia River. It is characteristic that from the village of Voraksino to the bridge by the village of Ovinishche, the forward edge, intersecting the river, crossed to the eastern side and ran along the edge of a small but dense forest. This was obviously done to make use of the hills which were located on the eastern bank of the Voloshnia River.

Considering the given axis as being secondary, the enemy deployed the fire means of the defense in one line. In all, on this sector there were 49 machine gun fire positions, 9 antitank defense guns, 10 weapons pits with overhead protection, and 28 dug-outs for 6–10 men each.

A smoothed-out road ran in the depth of the defense – a lateral line of communications where many 155mm shell cartridge cases were discovered. Obviously fire was conducted from roving guns here.

All structures were located 50–75 meters from one another, and the dug-outs located at a distance of 30–50 meters from them.

The fire position for one battery was located in the village of Ostashevo.

3. Strong Point Kobylevo–Churilovo–Afanasovo (Western Front)

For the given strong point, the design for German defense under winter conditions is characteristic (Sketch 7); here the means of defense are located exclusively in populated areas.

As is obvious from Sketch 7, the arrangement of fire means was dictated exclusively by the trace and location of the populated areas.

4. Strong Point – Dairy Farm (Southern Front)

The dairy farm, adapted as a strong point, was located on average rough terrain and had a number of structures and a railroad line passing through it (Sketch 8).

The fire structures at the strong point consisted of buildings adapted for defense. For example, casements were located inside and outside the buildings, using a foundation of rubble and a wall of brickwork. The casement walls and floors were dressed in boards, plank beds were set up for rest, and the casement itself was heated by a small portable metal stove. The casements had an overhead cover of 2 rows of rails laid 0.5–1 meter apart, 2 rows of ties, and dirt filler 0.5–0.75 meters thick. Such overhead cover protected

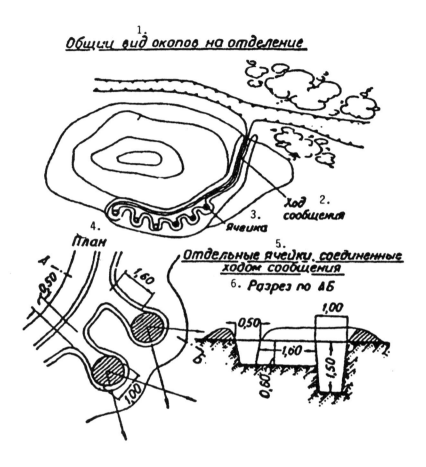

Sketch 11. Types of German trenches

1. Overall view of trenches in section
2. Communications trench
3. Foxhole
4. Plan
5. Individual foxholes joined by communications trench
6. Section along A-B

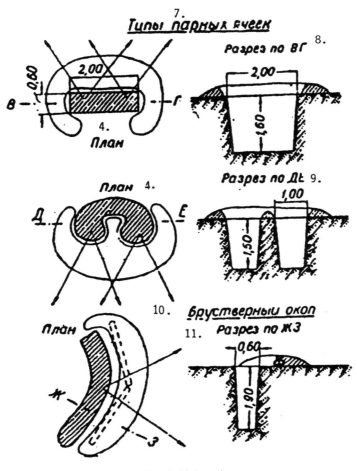

Sketch 11 (cont.)

7. Types of two-man foxholes
8. Section along V-G
9. Section along D-E
10. Raised trench
11. Section along Zh-Z

the Germans from direct hits by bombs and low-caliber artillery shells.

Within the building, full profile trenches were set up for medium machine guns, with embrasures in the walls (Sketch 9). One of the shortcomings of such a fire position was that, with a 3-brick wall thickness along the outer mouth, the embrasure was only 0.4 meters, which made it impossible for the fire position to have a supplementary fire sector. It was fairly common to encounter over fire points located in buildings an overhead cover made of one row of logs for protecting the man firing in case the building collapsed.

To set up the embrasure in domiciles or household structures, the enemy most often used window openings, and made openings in the walls as reserve exits from the shelters and as a means of conducting fire from antitank guns, for which trenches were sometimes set up. Right-angle embrasures, 15 × 35 centimeters or 20 × 60 centimeters, were made in stone and wooden walls. The embrasures were often set up along the corners of the building and teams servicing a machine gun or automatic weapons were located in the full profile trenches set up under the floor and adapted for defense of the houses. Very often light machine guns and, more rarely, medium machine guns were located in the garrets of buildings, for which openings in the tile or straw roofs were made.

The shelters (dug-outs) were set up in a primitive fashion, using the reverse slopes or the railroad embankment, and were usually camouflaged. Most often the overhead cover consisted of one row of logs or two rows of ties with around one meter of dirt filler, which protected the soldiers from bombs and low-caliber shells.

The principal shortcoming was that the dug-outs had a ceiling cover with a large span, so that the thrust of the logs and ties did not exceed 0.25 meters. This strongly reduced the resistance of the overhead cover.

Enemy observation points were set up on house roofs or in covered trenches with observation areas. Such trenches were set up on commanding heights and were well camouflaged on the background of the terrain. Observation slits were covered with ordinary window glass, which made it possible, even with heavy frost, to conduct normal observation.

The enemy arranged the earth-and-timber fire positions, making use of hills or, more often, embankments. Overhead cover was made from two rows of ties or logs with a 0.3-meter layer of straw and a one-meter dirt filler. This fully protected the soldiers from bombs and large shell fragments. The earth-and-timber fire positions, for the most part, had one embrasure and were armed with a medium machine gun and automatic weapons.

Machine gun fire positions with an overhead covering of 0.5–1 meter were dug out in the railroad embankment (Sketch 10). This achieved good camouflage, and the machine gun teams were protected from shell fragments and bomb hits.

IV. ENGINEER PREPARATION OF THE ENEMY FIELD DEFENSE ZONE

In the engineer preparation of the terrain, the enemy widely and thoroughly uses domicile and farm structures, road embankments and fences. He builds special fire structures or adapts existing ones for medium and light machine guns, automatic weapons, and guns. The Germans build shelters for squads, more rarely for platoons, and arrange them on the reverse slopes of heights; some of the shelters are adapted for conducting fire; the enemy makes entrances into the shelter on the side of the attacker for more rapid readiness of infantry subunits for battle. The Germans deploy communication trenches as densely as possible, depending on available time and terrain. They bury tanks in the ground to reinforce the defense, thus turning them into permanent fire positions.

All German field defensive structures are exclusively earth-and-timber, and the overwhelming majority are the light type. Types of German trenches are shown in Sketch 11. Heavy defensive structures are rarely encountered, most often in the northwest and north. Instances of using concrete and reinforced concrete for field defensive structures were not noted.

The Germans use 2–3 stakes of barbed wire barriers; barbed wire braiding around trees, houses, and fences; knife rests concertina wire; and trip wires as anti-personnel obstacles.

Barriers in the forests and on roads are also encountered. In the winter they use iced slopes. As a rule, the Germans mine all barbed wire obstacles and barriers with fougasse, booby traps, anti-personnel, and, more rarely, antitank mines.

In addition, the Germans set up anti-personnel mines to protect the mined antitank fields; individual areas mined only with anti-personnel mines were also encountered.

The Germans widely use various antitank mines and high explosives as antitank obstacles, setting up mine fields on tankable directions. It should be particularly noted that the Germans mine fields not only on the defense but also on the offense to rapidly reinforce captured terrain.

One can judge the scale of mine obstacles from the fact that in the zone of the 37th Army, as many as 15,000 enemy mines and high explosive booby traps were extracted in the course of three months.

The mining of fields on a broad scale strengthened the German defense and made it more resistant.

All obstacles, both anti-personnel and antitank, are arranged by the Germans so as to be covered by fire. Mine fields are usually arranged 200–500 meters from the forward edge of the defense. No system in setting up mines within the limits of the mine field was observed; mines are usually placed in a disordered fashion.

The Germans widely use booby traps, which they set up in dug-outs, in domiciles, and in materiel left behind; corpses of their own soldiers are also mined.

The Germans widely use the local population for defensive work; they use their own sapper units in battle together with infantry, and during crisis periods the sappers are even used as infantry.

One should particularly look at the Germans' use of populated areas for defense.

Each populated area is turned into a strong point by means of adapting individual buildings for the defense and building additional structures, creating an all-round system of defense.

The forward edge of the defense, as a rule, does not run along the outskirts of the populated area, but is brought out somewhat forward, approximately 150–200 meters.

The projecting contours of the populated area are used for flanking.

In addition to erecting conventional field-type fire structures, the enemy turns necessary houses, barns, and other structures into fire positions; all other structures which hinder the conduct of fire are usually burned.

The most common adaptation of a building for defense is deepening the basement under the shelter, chopping through an embrasure in the foundation, and strengthening the overhead cover of the basement with a roof beam and dirt.

The Germans also set up shelters in basements, under houses, and in barns. In houses, especially stone houses, embrasures are simply made in the wall; windows and doors may be adapted as embrasures. They also adapt barns and domiciles for guns. To do this they break one wall of the building and roll in the guns.

Garrets are very often used by the Germans as fire positions for automatic weapons and machine guns.

They enmesh roads with barbed wire, intercept them with knife rests, and sometimes dig deep ditches across them.

Mortars are, as a rule, set up on open positions and behind buildings on the rear outskirts of populated areas. Shelters are set up for the team.

CONCLUSION

Practical combat experience of Red Army units has shown that on the defense the Germans more strongly cover the primary roads and road junctions, including populated areas in their defensive zone.

In organizing the defense, the Germans structure it according to the principle of protecting, in the first order, the primary direction.

In structuring their defense on a base of strong points and centers of resistance, the Germans prepare them for a long, all-round stubborn defense. Sealed off garrisons do not, as a rule, surrender, but, on the contrary, the German command supports in every way possible the dispatching of reserves, ammunition, and food from the air.

These positive aspects of the German defense, as a consequence of its brokenness, unavoidably give rise to its weak aspects as well. The weak aspects of the German defense are the secondary directions and gaps between strong points and centers of resistance.

In organizing an offensive against a German defense, it is necessary to adhere to the following:

1. Searching out and determining weak areas (directions) in the enemy defense by careful reconnaissance.
2. After finding them, covertly and carefully preparing a strike against the weak areas; boldly penetrating into the enemy defense, widely using strikes on the flank and rear of the strong points.
3. While organizing deep and shallow envelopments for the purpose of striking the flank and rear of the strong points during the penetration, always immobilizing the enemy from the front and suppressing defensive strong points; otherwise the danger of falling into a "fire sack" may arise.
4. Always taking into consideration the action of the German defense and the Germans' wide use of counterattacks supported by tanks and aviation. Therefore, the main condition for success of the breakthrough of the defense is rapid consolidation of captured terrain and constant readiness of troops to repel enemy counterattacks.
5. Not sealing off a surrounded German defense garrison in the hopes of taking prisoners; instead quickly and carefully preparing a strike against them for the purpose of completely destroying the enemy, who has refused to surrender.
6. Always keeping in mind that the Germans use the terrain well and primarily reinforce it by means of a field fortification, broadly adapting populated areas and terrain objects for the defense.

German Use of Antiaircraft Artillery for Firing against Ground Targets

Lately on a number of sectors of the front, the German command has been forced to use antiaircraft artillery to fight against ground targets, reinforcing, by this, insufficient artillery means in the offensive. The broadest use of antiaircraft artillery by the Germans against ground targets took place during the offensive against Sevastopol' in June 1942. Judging from German documents lately captured by our units, the Germans rather highly valued the actions of antiaircraft guns (especially heavy ones) against ground targets, emphasizing their significant destructive force, even when firing against strongly fortified structures having reinforced concrete cover.

In the German document, "Report on the Combat Actions of the Antiaircraft Artillery Group 'North' for the Period 28 May–25 June 1942," the preparation for the offensive and actions of this group during the offensive against Severnaia Bukhta near Sevastopol' are described in detail.

The decision to use antiaircraft artillery in the ground battle was made by the command of the 8th Air Corps to aid aviation in resolving its missions on the battlefield and decisively support ground troops in overcoming earth-and-timber fire positions and other strongly fortified structures. For this purpose a significant portion of the antiaircraft artillery located in the Crimea was withdrawn from subordination to the 10th Antiaircraft Division and attached directly to the 8th Air Corps; a representative of the 10th Antiaircraft Division was located at the headquarters of the latter. For convenience of control, the antiaircraft artillery resubordinated to the air corps was divided into combat groups, each consisting of several light and heavy batteries.

The following missions were assigned to the antiaircraft artillery combat group "North," which consisted of 3 heavy batteries (12 88mm guns) and 3 light batteries (1 battery with 9 37mm cannons and 2 batteries with 15 20mm cannons):

- support the advance of the 54th Army Corps by massed ground fire of the heavy batteries;

70

- destroy permanent fire positions and strongly fortified structures in the zone of the corps offensive;
- hold the enemy in the depth of his defense from advanced positions, interacting with the heavy batteries of 2 antiaircraft artillery combat groups;
- cover the large massing of their own troops while they occupy the staging area; cover artillery which has advanced forward from attacks of low-flying aircraft.

From 28 May to 6 June inclusive, preparation for the offensive was conducted.

On 28–29 May, the commander of combat group "North" arranged in detail all issues concerning the forthcoming offensive with the commander of the 54th Army Corps and the commanders of the infantry divisions that were part of the corps (132d, 22d, 50th, and 24th Infantry Divisions), after which he carefully reconnoitered the terrain; on 30 May he presented a plan for conducting the battle to the commander of the air corps.

The battle plan foresaw attaching light antiaircraft artillery by batteries to the 132d, 22d, and 50th Infantry Divisions; the commander of the combat group proposed to use the heavy batteries in a centralized fashion.

From 31 May to 2 June, after the assignment of the missions to the battery commanders, the latter conducted reconnaissance, studied the terrain, equipped the fire positions and observation points, established communications with the infantry divisions, and refined the forthcoming missions with them.

Particular attention during this period was given to the selection and preparation of fire positions and observation points, and to the development of a detailed communications plan. The commander of the combat group was directly in charge of the selection and preparation of the fire positions and observation points.

For the purpose of implementing uninterrupted communications in battle, in addition to wire means the group was reinforced with eight "B"-type radios. To support the conduct of several groups of concentrated fire by the heavy batteries against particularly important targets, telephone and radio communications with all combat groups were established by the communications regiment of the air corps.

On 3 June, heavy batteries (88mm) went over to the initial fire positions near the front and, after occupying the prepared observation points, began to reconnoiter enemy fire positions.

On 4 June the command post of the combat group was transferred to

71

a new location, and the commander of the air corps met with all group and battery commanders concerning forthcoming missions.

Beginning on 4 June, the heavy batteries, having reconnaissance data concerning the fire positions, conducted a ranging on the important targets. The light batteries covered the supply path from air attack until 5 June. On 5 June the batteries went over to new fire positions, having occupied them in the area of action of the infantry divisions with whom they were to interact in battle.

After such careful preparation there followed a five-day artillery preparation by all artillery means; only after this did the infantry offensive begin.

The iron stability of our defense at Sevastopol' should be noted. In the "Report" the beginning of the offensive is described in the following way:

> The ground forces advanced with artillery used for the first time in such quantity and force in the German army. From guns of various calibers, beginning with mortars and ending with the heaviest guns in the world (on railroad mounts), artillery preparation against enemy fortifications is conducted for five days, at the conclusion of which a massed fire strike of all guns, including all light batteries of the antiaircraft artillery group, is conducted at 0300 on 7 June. Under cover of this rapid fire burst, the divisions of the 54th Army Corps advance. The offensive, however, comes against a deliberately equipped, strongly mined defensive system of positions, as well as Bolshevik obstinacy. Uninterrupted destructive enemy artillery fire is conducted against all German positions. It prevents the observation points from functioning, complicates the actions of the fire positions, and minute by minute disrupts the branch telephone network.

The document goes on further to say, "The first days of the battles showed that under this hellish enemy artillery fire it is impossible to conduct the offensive further." Thus, beginning on 10 June, the heavy batteries once again suppress enemy artillery.

During the entire period of the offensive, light antiaircraft batteries interacted with infantry divisions, supporting, in platoons, the advance of the regiments and repelling the aircraft attack.

Heavy batteries were used exclusively in a centralized fashion by the commander of the combat group. In individual cases, heavy batteries of some combat groups were united in the hands of a single commander, specifically, the commander of the 14th Antiaircraft Artillery Regiment, who concentrated their fire on one or another important target. The major aims of the heavy antiaircraft artillery batteries were destroying permanent fire and earth-and-timber fire positions and other fortified structures, suppressing artillery, fighting against naval vessels and ships, and firing against air fields and towns by means of incendiary shells.

The "Report" noted the extremely rapid opening and concentration of fire against the necessary targets, which assured the presence of precise and uninterruptedly operating means of communication, i.e., telephone and, especially, radio, and a branched network of observation points.

The method of putting the advancing forward troops in front of the observer, who, by radio from capably chosen observation points, directed heavy battery fire, merits attention. In addition, corrector aircraft and tracer rounds were widely used to control fire.

The "Report" noted the high effectiveness, from the point of view of accuracy and the destructive force of the shells, of firing against ground targets from 88mm antiaircraft guns. Thus, among the permanent fire positions destroyed were five with armored cover and a very strongly fortified structure in the Bel'bek Valley (an antiaircraft artillery shelter).

It is important to note the good organization of gun repair. The "Report" states that directly at the fire positions, in the course of the entire period of the offensive, day and night, grooves were ground, breech mechanisms were corrected, and other repair work done. In addition, during the period of the indicated battles, i.e., 28 May – 26 June, 17 88mm guns, 18 20mm guns, and one antiaircraft director were restored, and 11 barrels were replaced in the ordnance workshop of the antiaircraft artillery combat group.

From the summarized content of the report on the combat actions of the German antiaircraft artillery combat group "North," it is useful to draw the following conclusions:

1. Antiaircraft artillery, in the absence of the necessary quantity of artillery means, and under conditions of weak enemy pressure from the air, may be used to fight against ground targets.

2. The targets for antiaircraft artillery may be not only crowds of infantry, fire points, etc., but also permanent and earth-and-timber enemy fire positions which do not have large reinforced concrete cover.

3. A broad network of observation points and a communications network worked out in detail, with broad use of radio means, provide uninterrupted control of artillery fire under the most complex conditions.

4. Well-organized gun repair in the immediate vicinity of the battlefield is a necessary condition for increasing the survivability of artillery materiel. If there had not been an artillery workshop working at full capacity to restore guns, then in the first days of the offensive combat group "North" would have lost its combat capability due to the absence of materiel in good repair.

On the Issue of Studying War Experience

In the course of the war, tactical procedures for conducting battle, tactical-technical procedures, and methods for using tactical means in battle are continually changing and improving.

A year of war introduced a number of new operational-tactical procedures for the struggle, making it possible to annihilate the enemy more assuredly with the least loss of forces and a minimum of sacrifices.

There have been especially great changes in tactical procedures for using technical means. Each day of battle, even individual battles, introduces a new, sometimes radically changing concept of the possibilities of using one or another means for fighting.

Quite recently, in the course of the war, antitank weapons appeared. Having mastered them, the troops found in them a reliable means for fighting against tanks. And not so long ago they were used in the fight against aircraft, also with good results; now their use by troops against enemy aircraft is the rule. The latter days of battle have shown that antitank weapons were an effective means of destroying earth-and-timber fire positions as well.

This is only one of many instances of changes engendered by the war. Each of them, individually taken, is of great value to the troops, since it broadens the field of action for using one or another means for fighting, reduces its dead time in battle, and increases the overall saturation of the battle with dynamic means of fighting.

Many new tactical procedures of troops and technical means of fighting engendered by the war have become the property of the entire Red Army and have rendered great assistance in the struggle against the enemy. But many new procedures obtained in the process of battle, undoubtedly valuable for the troops, have not received rapid and broad dissemination, only because issues concerning the generalization of experience and, especially, its exchange among units and formations, are very poorly dealt with in formations and even in *fronts*.

It is usually accepted to consider under the topic of the study of experience the investigation of one or another procedure for fighting which has arisen in

75

battle, and the development of documents for the troops on the basis of this. In principle this is true, but in order to investigate thoroughly and come to a definite conclusion on the expediency of the broad use of a new procedure for fighting, one instance (experience) is usually not sufficient. Repeated use of this procedure (sometimes many times) is required. Here, then, is a wide field of activity for commanders at all levels and their staffs.

A device which has been used once, and which has given positive results in battle, will be repeated over a period of time most often by the one who used it for the first time. But this will take place when, on a sector of a given front, specific conditions unfold which resemble the first instance of the use of the given procedure. A mistake of many people is in patiently waiting for a repetition of a procedure used once, without attempts to bring it to other sectors of the front where the necessary conditions, perhaps, are already available; if they are not, then they will be created on a number of sectors of the front more rapidly than on one. Document development with corresponding conclusions is not required for this; only brief unit information with a brief description of the procedure, combat conditions under which it was used, and results achieved is necessary.

Such broad and continually active information for units and formations should be organized by army and *front* staffs. It is of great assistance in the matter of studying combat experience, and will also make it possible for units to rapidly seize and use in battle everything valuable which arises in the combat situation over the large expanse of the front. This information should be considered a most important part of the study and exchange of combat experience.

One should not study the combat experience of one's own troops isolated from the study of enemy tactical procedures for fighting and new technical means used by him. This work is no less important, making it possible to render reliable counteraction against enemy tactics and equipment; it should be carried out together with the study of the combat experience of one's own troops. Everything new in enemy methods and procedures being used, obtained directly in battle, by prisoner interrogation, or by any other means, should be rapidly transmitted to the troops by means of information.

One of the most successful forms of unit and formation information about new tactical procedures for fighting, both of one's own troops and enemy troops, is the use of the "Information Leaflets." Thus, for example, such a leaflet with the stamp "For Service Use" was issued three to four times a month by the chief of the engineer troops of the southwestern direction, and distributed to all engineer units, one leaflet per company.

The "Information Leaflet" contains the following:

- unit information about new tactical-technical procedures for one's own troops in fighting;
- warning about enemy use of new means and procedures for fighting;
- instructions from the chief of engineer troops to subordinate units;
- characteristic combat episodes from the lives of engineer troops.

One of the "Information Leaflets" of the chief of the engineer troops of the southwestern direction is given below as a model.

Death To The German Invaders!

For Service Use

Chief Of Engineer Troops of the Southwestern Direction

Information Leaflet   13

1

In the German army, engineer troops are divided into engineer-combat units, which are sapper troops, and military-construction units consisting of construction battalions.

The sapper units directly participate in the battle, making possible the advance of their own troops in the offense and the repulsion of attacks in the defense.

All instructions and directions of the German army require tight communications and interaction of the sappers with other combat arms, their concentrated use, and assignment of missions in advance.

In the first months of the war, the German army had a sufficient quantity of engineer equipment and trained sapper personnel. These personnel, by now, are disoriented and poorly replenished, since the insufficiency of reserves compels the German command to use sappers as infantry.

2

To attack fortified lines, the Germans created special blocking detachments (infantry, tanks, sappers, artillerymen). There were 30–40 sappers in the detachment, divided into two groups: assault and reserve.

The assault group was divided into four subgroups.

The first subgroup was a shock subgroup (four to five men) armed with rifles, grenades, and wire cutters.

The second subgroup, a smoke subgroup, was assigned to set up smoke screens during the approach of the demolition and flame-thrower groups to the earth-and-timber or permanent fire positions. They were armed with rifles, grenades, and smoke pots.

The third subgroup was a demolition subgroup (5–6 men), armed with rifles, hand grenades, and 3kg explosive charges.

The fourth subgroup was a flame-thrower subgroup (7–8 men) armed with rifles and flame-throwers.

A reserve of around 10–15 men was divided into 3 subgroups: strike, smoke, and demolition.

The sapper blocking detachment advanced in small rushes under cover of artillery, mortar, and machine gun fire.

3

It has been established by previous war experience that our earth-and-timber and permanent fire positions were rapidly adapted for defense by the Germans. For this they used entrances for embrasures and dug out new embrasures. Reinforced concrete points were often turned into mortar fire positions, for which apertures were cut out in the point cover with the help of the sappers' special mechanical instruments.

4

In attacking earth-and-timber fire positions, the Germans used gasoline, which was poured through ventilation pipes and other openings inside the fire positions. A short time later, when gasoline vapor filled the area, hand grenades were thrown in, causing an explosion.

5

Unable to withstand the pressure of our advancing troops, the fascists increased the number of explosive obstacles on the approaches to their positions.

Thus, Colonel Goldovich's sappers, in clearing the mines from one of the enemy centers of resistance (a populated area), encountered the following system of obstacles: on all sides the populated area was belted by mine fields. Antitank mines were set up in 2–3 rows in a checkerboard fashion. The distance between mines and rows was 3–4 meters. Behind the antitank mine field was an anti-personnel field of C-35 mines in 2 rows. The distance between mines was 4–6 meters, and between rows 3–6 meters.

In tank-proof areas, anti-personnel mine fields consisted of 3 rows. The last row of mines was located in the immediate vicinity of the fire positions. Booby traps with charges of TNT, demolition slabs and grenades were used in the mine field. All houses and domestic structures, including demolished ones, were mined.

Mining means were varied. For example, inside a room on the wall beside the door, 14 200g TNT charges were laid. A pressure fuse was screwed into one of them. Wire was attached to the door, causing an explosion when it was opened.

A cluster of hand grenades was placed in a stove. A wire was tied to one of the grenades behind a retaining ball. The cluster was fastened by wire behind the iron cover of the stove. When the door was opened, there was an explosion.

The entrance to the potato cellar was mined by a kilogram charge with a pressure fuse hidden under a wooden step. The charge with pressure fuse was set up in a pile of potatoes. The wire went into the potatoes and was fastened to the cellar walls. Upon entrance to the cellar, there was an explosion. When the potatoes were sorted, there was also an explosion.

In front of the entrance to the building there was a box of cartridges in which as many as 30 TNT demolition charges were placed. A pressure fuse was screwed into one of the charges. Carefully camouflaged wire was fastened to the door of the building, and when the door was opened, there was an explosion.

On a bed was a chair, from the legs of which a trip wire ran into the mattress. In the mattress was a charge of 6 TNT demolition charges with a pressure fuse; there was an explosion when the chair was removed.

A gramophone was mined in one of the houses. A kilogram charge with a pressure fuse was located half a meter from the gramophone, as was one under the gramophone. An explosion occurred with pressure on the gramophone or with shifting it.

Boards piled in disorder within a room were mined with a charge with a pressure fuse. An explosion occurred when the boards were sorted.

There was an iron bed in front of an apartment door. A wire ran from one of the legs of the bed to the charge, which was fastened in the corner of the room. The charge and wire were carefully camouflaged.

On a table were two uncamouflaged charges, each three kilograms, with a pressure fuse; around the table were six pressure booby traps, carefully camouflaged.

In one house on the wall was a German gas mask. In a case, instead of a gas mask there were several grenades; a fuse from one of them was fastened to the top of the case. When the case was opened there was an explosion. A sapper who opened the gas mask heard a hissing. Without losing his presence of mind, he threw it away and darted out of the house. Three seconds later there was an explosion.

There were as many as 30 booby traps in individual houses. The care in camouflaging and the variety of booby traps should be noted. All mine fields, high explosives, and booby traps were removed without a single loss on the part of the sappers.

These examples show that in the future we will encounter an increasing number of explosive obstacles. It is necessary in all engineer units to steadfastly conduct training on demolition-clearing operations and educate bold and experienced demolition sappers. Our work in this direction is especially necessary and valuable for troops, because it protects the lives of our soldiers and facilitates a more rapid rout of fascism.

6

Enemy artillery shells captured by our units can be used as mines for setting up obstacles, especially when attached to captured positions. For this purpose one can use only high explosive and fragmentation shells.

To use an artillery shell as a mine, it is necessary to do the following:

- unscrew the shell fuse or fuse-hole plug;
- fill the fuse sleeve (eye) with an explosive material;
- place and fasten the capsule-detonator with an all-purpose fuse or general purpose mine fuse.

The fuse and fuse-hole plug are unscrewed with a special wrench or opener. While unscrewing the fuse, the shell is gripped in a wooden vise. The work is done by two soldiers. It is necessary to do the unscrewing observing measures of extreme caution. The following are forbidden during this work:

- striking the handle of the wrench with a hammer or other object;

- having people who are not required for the work in the area;
- having other shells in the work area.

If the fuse is attached by an anchoring screw, that is first unscrewed, then the fuse.

A borehole TNT charge (when the sleeve/eye is of large dimensions) or powdered TNT (when the sleeve/eye is of small dimensions) is placed in the fuse sleeve/eye. The borehole charge in the sleeve is reinforced by pegs; powdered explosives are jammed in by means of oakum or rags.

The fuse (capsule-detonator and general purpose mine fuse) which has been placed in the fuse charge is reinforced so that the fuse does not shift when the cotter pin is pulled out.

The filling of the mines is done from the side. The mine-shells are placed horizontally in a trap, with the fuse's cotter pin pointed upwards. The depth of the trap is about 15 centimeters. A thin trip wire is fastened to a peg at a distance of 4–6 meters from the mine; the other end of the wire is fastened to the cotter pin of the general purpose mine fuse. The wire is loosely placed on pegs at a height of 10–15 centimeters above the ground.

Setting up the mines by one sapper requires around five minutes.

7

Lieutenant Colonel Khvostov's sappers removed the following over 26 days: 981 antitank mines and 28 high explosives; to reinforce captured lines, the following were set up: 3,395 antitank mines, 83 high explosives, and 160 anti-personnel mines. In these battles, Major Zavodsky's sapper group blocked the German shelters, killing four fascists. Sapper Gorbachev set up 80 mines in three hours under enemy fire.

8

The sapper-demolition group under the command of Junior Lieutenant Kislev, under strong enemy machine gun and mortar fire, blew up a railroad bed, preventing the passage of an enemy armored train.

9

Major Ovsiannitsky's sappers, under the command of Lieutenant Poretsky, in supporting the attack of tanks under enemy fire, cleared three obstacles by disarming 34 antitank mines.

10

Lieutenant Zhirov's sappers constructed a dummy airfield which enemy aviation intensively bombed.

11

The sappers of Major Ovsiannitsky and Lieutenant Korostelev dynamically operated in the enemy rear. At the end of April, important roads were mined and a bridge was blown up by sapper-commando groups. Vehicles with ammunition were blown up on mines. Sergeant Arakelov and Red Army soldier Posukashvili distinguished themselves in these actions.

12

Major Kozhevnikov's sappers, in the course of 12 days on stony ground and under enemy artillery fire, dug out 80 full-profile trenches with communication trenches, and constructed 26 earth-and-timber fire positions. This work received a good evaluation from the commander of the unit, Hero of the Soviet Union Major-General Pravalov.

13

In clearing a mine field, a commando-sapper from Lieutenant Colonel Makhin's units stepped on a C-35 mine, which exploded. The sapper managed to lie down and was unharmed. A Red Army soldier 25 meters from the mine was wounded.

14

The sapper platoon under the command of Lieutenant Napotvoridze, while carrying out its mission to create a defense center, was attacked by superior fascist forces. Having occupied the line of defense, the sappers approached the enemy at close range and, by means of friendly rifle and captured machine gun fire, sent the fascists fleeing. The enemy left 8 bodies behind.

INSTRUCTIONS OF THE GENERAL STAFF OF THE RED ARMY
on the use of articles 16–19, "Regulations for Staff Field
Service, 1942" in formations, armies, fronts, and military districts

(directive of the General Staff of the Red Army 1005058, dated 2 August 1942)

In the staffs of large formations instances of incorrect interrelations of chiefs of combat arms (deputy commanders) with chiefs of combined arms staffs have been observed. Some deputy commanders and commanders are inclined to examine the question of interrelationships exclusively from the point of view of subordination, to the detriment of the interests of the overall matter of troop control.

It was established that at the foundation of the irregularities in interrelations lies the incorrect use in practice of articles 16–19 of the "Regulations for Staff Field Service, 1942" by chiefs of army and *front* staffs and by deputy commanders as chiefs of combat arms.

The following is given as clarification:

1. The chief of staff is the deputy commander, and only he has the right to issue instructions in the name of the commander.
2. Chiefs of combat arms who are deputy commanders, and chiefs of services implement leadership of special units and services on order of the Military Council (commander).
3. Chiefs of combat arms, the chief of the rear (deputy rear commander), and chiefs of services are obliged to continually keep the chief of staff well informed of the measures being carried out by them on supporting the decisions of the commander.
4. The chief of staff is obliged to report promptly to the deputy commanders on all changes in the situation and on combat instructions issued by headquarters.
5. Staffs of the chiefs of combat arms and the chief of the rear should work in complete cooperation with army (*front*) headquarters.

    The distribution of work between commanders of the combined arms staff should be such that each of them knows with which functionary from the staff of the chief of the combat arm he is coupled in his work, and to which commanders in the combined arms headquarters he must turn in the field of joint work.
6. The current instructions are subject to guidance pending refinement of articles 16–19, "Regulations for Staff Field Service."

INDEX OF
PROPER NAMES